100

THINGS TO DO IN
COLUMBIA, MO
BEFORE YOU
DIE

100

THINGS TO DO IN
COLUMBIA, MO
BEFORE YOU
DIE

• •

STEPHEN PAUL SAYERS

Permissions may be sought directly from Reedy Press at the above mailing address or via our website at www.reedypress.com.

Library of Congress Control Number: 2022936991

ISBN: 9781681063836

Design by Jill Halpin

Cover image and all interior images courtesy of L. G. Patterson.

Printed in the United States of America
22 23 24 25 26   5 4 3 2 1

CONTENTS

● ●

• •

Music and Entertainment

• •

vii

Sports and Recreation

Culture and History

• •

• •

• •

PREFACE

I have a confession to make. Twenty years ago, this New Englander had to check a map of the United States to find out where Missouri was. Now, I could chalk up my geographic ignorance to a crumbling public education system, or the melting of the polar ice caps, but it's time to come clean: I had a bit of an East Coast bias. I was brought up believing that anything between the East and West Coasts was just a flyover state.

I was wrong.

Driving from Lambert-St. Louis airport to a job interview at the University of Missouri in Columbia in the spring of 2003, I experienced a visual assault the likes of which I had never seen: lavender pinks and deep magentas of redbud trees peeking out from the lush, wooded green; and deep, earthy-chocolate soil scattered with henbit blanketing the endless miles of farmland. By the time I rumbled into Columbia, the entire town was abloom in a vibrant mid-April explosion of color.

I was falling in love.

Twenty years later, I'm still in love, and this book pays homage to the place my family and I call home. This account is not necessarily a "best of Columbia" list, but a list of what makes COMO a unique, one-of-a-kind experience—and one of the coolest places on any map.

● ●

Please join me and other readers on my Facebook page, 100ThingsCOMO, and let me know which selections on the list you liked as well as others you think I should have included. I welcome the different perspectives that will add to future editions. Together, we'll get it right!

Stephen Paul Sayers

• •

ACKNOWLEDGMENTS

My deepest appreciation to every shopkeeper who let me skulk through their place of business—and were polite enough not to ask me to leave! Thanks to every restauranteur, business owner, and city staffer who answered my questions or responded to my multiple emails. Thanks to all who offered their unique perspectives on Columbia, especially L. G. and Melissa Patterson for sending me to places I didn't even know existed. Now I do, and you will, too! Special thanks to L. G. Patterson, who contributed the photographs to this book. His skillful eye has helped me tell the story of Columbia with a little more texture.

FOOD AND DRINK

BURGER UP
AT BOOCHES

Rated as one of the top 10 burgers in America by *USA Today* and among the best college-town food by *Sports Illustrated*, Booches Billiard Hall has been a Columbia tradition since 1884. "Club La Booche" is no-frills dining at its best—think 100-year-old tables, vintage neon beer signs, and burgers served on wax paper. The only thing served in a dish is their chili, but you won't get it unless you ask for a "bowl of red." And don't ask for fries. They only serve Backer's chips, a local favorite. For the old-school billiard crowd, Booches is one of the only places in town that still has snooker tables. Keep an eye out for the brass plaques on the bar commemorating a dearly departed patron's favorite perch. Located on 9th Street since 1928, Booches remains closed on Sundays, with a reminder in the window: "See you in church."

110 S 9th St., (573) 874-9519
booches1884.com

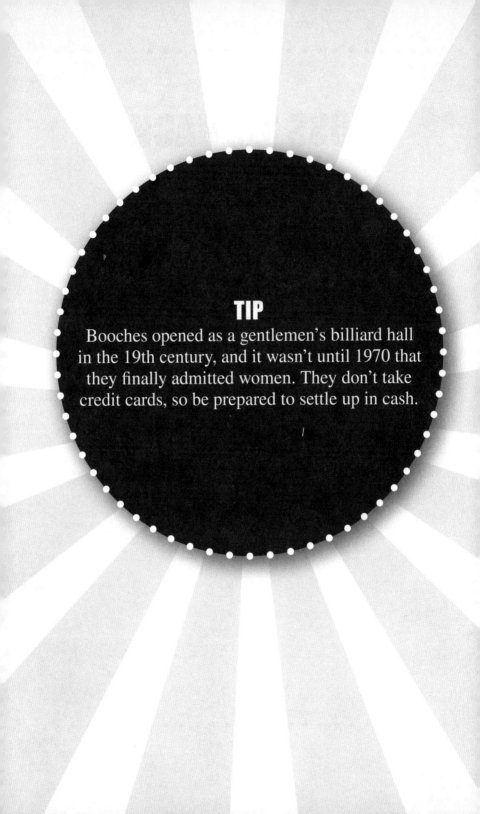

TIP

Booches opened as a gentlemen's billiard hall in the 19th century, and it wasn't until 1970 that they finally admitted women. They don't take credit cards, so be prepared to settle up in cash.

TOSS 'EM BACK
AT "THE BERG"

If you're looking for trendy, this watering hole isn't for you. A favorite of the Mizzou community since 1963, the Heidelberg is a happy-hour haven for students and professors alike. I mean, who doesn't love dark wood, brick walls, draft specials, and BOGO apps. Revered by its Columbia patrons, the Berg was actually looted for bricks and souvenirs when it burned to the ground in 2003. Rebuilt in 2004, the Berg's high-backed wooden booths still aren't the most comfortable, but they give you quiet and privacy, even when the place is getting loud. The menu features burgers, wings, salads, and wraps that will hit the spot. When the weather's nice, take a hike up to the rooftop bar and soak up the afternoon sun, or hang around for a drink under the stars.

420 S 9th St., (573) 449-6927
theheidelberg.com

BELLY UP
AT THE BROADWAY DINER

This family-run establishment has been a downtown staple for late-night meals and early breakfasts since 1938. The Diner's retro vibe checkerboard tiled floor, colorful cushioned booths, and swivel bar stools have hosted the likes of Bill Haley and His Comets and *Jeopardy* host Alex Trebek. The place might be a bit cramped, but if you can't find a seat at the counter, someone will eventually wave you over to join them in their booth. They say you haven't eaten at the Broadway Diner until you've tried the Stretch—hash browns topped with scrambled eggs covered in chili, cheddar cheese, and veggies—or Matt's Dilemma (the Stretch minus the veggies, but with sausage and gravy instead of chili). See the dilemma? Try 'em both and you've truly experienced the Broadway Diner.

22 S 4th St., (573) 875-1173
broadwaydinercomo.com

TIP
The diner gets busy on the weekend, so get there early if you want to avoid a line out the door.

HAVE A SLICE
AT SHAKESPEARE'S

Shakespeare's is *the* go-to pizza in Columbia, serving up the best homemade, hand-tossed pies in mid-Missouri since 1973. The pizza isn't always pretty. Sometimes the toppings veer to the left or right, or the sauce encroaches too far onto the crust, but that's what makes it Shakespeare's. Try the "Masterpiece," winner of *Good Morning America*'s 2010 Best Bites Challenge: College Edition. Or just build your own with white, wheat, or gluten-free crust and a variety of mouthwatering toppings. Grab your washcloth napkins and silverware as you take in the eclectic, Route 66–style retro décor. Shakespeare's is loud and festive, with staff tossing dough to lines of waiting children or inventing creative ways to call out your pizza order. Grab some dough-to-go for a pizza at home or a frozen pie if you're in a hurry.

225 S 9th St., (573) 449-2454
3304 W Broadway, (573) 447-1202
3911 Peachtree Dr., (573) 447-7435
shakespeares.com

TIP

Pick up a frozen Shakespeare's Pizza at grocery stores and markets throughout Missouri (including Hy-Vee Grocery Store, Gerbes Super Market, and Schnucks Markets). They can also ship out of state if you simply can't live without it!

OTHER LOCAL PIZZA PLACES

G & D Pizzaria
2101 W Broadway, Crossroads West Shopping Center
(573) 445-8336
gdpizzasteak.com

Southside Pizza and Pub
3908 Peach Tree Dr., (573) 256-7337
southsidepizzacomo.com

Pizza Tree
900 Cherry St., (573) 874-9925
pizzatreepizza.com

Gumby's Pizza
1201 E Broadway, (573) 874-8629
gumbyscolumbia.com

Angelo's Pizza and Steak House
4107 S Providence Rd., (573) 443-6100
angelospizzaandsteak.com

SNAP TO THE JAZZ
AT MURRY'S

With live jazz to compliment a great atmosphere, Murry's has always been the ultimate in cool. They don't advertise, and you can't call ahead for a table. Everyone waits in line, including one former governor and his staff, who were once refused a reservation. Murry's motto is "keep it simple, make it good," and they've followed through on that promise for 35 years. The menu is best described as eclectic American, with traditional appetizers, salads, sandwiches, meats, and sides done with a creative flair. And don't miss the onion rings! The jazz lineup is top-notch, with piano Jazz from Monday to Thursday and trios on Saturday. They also host select jazz musicians through the community's "We Always Swing Jazz Series." Make plans to swing by this Columbia institution and experience what everyone's been raving about for more than a generation.

3107 Green Meadows Way, (573) 442-4969
murrysrestaurant.net

ORDER UP SOME CHOPPED COW
AT ERNIE'S

Ernie's Café and Steak House has been around since 1934 and has served breakfast and lunch at its Walnut Street location since 1946. This Columbia classic is a meat-lovers paradise, with plenty of steak, pork, and burger options to satisfy any Midwest palate. *Dick Tracy* artist and creator Chester Gould was such a fan of the "chopped cow" that he sketched an original art mural that still adorns Ernie's wall. A perennial winner of "Best Breakfast" by *Inside Columbia* magazine, Ernie's has retained its cool, art-deco, historic charm, with classic neon lighting, black-and-white checkerboard flooring, vintage bar stools, and an extended wall-length booth that places you beside soon-to-be new friends on any given day. When the weather's warm, take it outside to the sidewalk patio for some people-watching.

1005 E Walnut St., (573) 874-7804
erniescolumbia.com

CARVE OUT SOME HISTORY
AT THE SHACK

The Shack has a storied history, having evolved from an old sandwich cart and burger joint in the 1920s and 1930s to a legendary campus watering hole. Its high-backed wooden booths and bar once bore the carvings and initials of thousands, including *Beetle Bailey* comic strip creator, Mort Walker, who immortalized the Shack in his cartoons. It's even rumored that the 1956 hit song "The Green Door," written by Mizzou alum Jim Lowe, was a tribute to the joint's verdant hue. The Shack burned to the ground in 1988, but a nostalgic re-creation is located at the Mizzou Student Unions, with wood salvaged from the original and walls that bear a new generation's carvings. If you long for some Columbia lore, grab your jackknife, visit the Shack, and be a part of its history.

MU Student Center
901 Rollins St., (573) 882-5493
unions.missouri.edu/space-the-shack

GUZZLE SOME SUDS
AT HARPO'S

You haven't experienced Columbia until you've elbowed through the Harpo's Bar and Grill crowd for a beer and burger on a Mizzou football game day. This iconic downtown college bar and grill has been the site of numerous postgame celebrations, often the final stop for joyous Tiger fans parading through the streets with goalposts ripped from Faurot Field. Even after 50 years in business, Harpo's still has lines of college students clamoring to gain entrance on weekend nights. It's also one of the best places in town to watch sports, with 30 TVs, a good selection of burgers and pub food, and six full-service bars. Make sure to visit the year-round rooftop bar with its two fire pits and a private lounge overlooking 10th and Cherry Streets. It's a worthy destination for Mizzou students, graduates, and anyone looking for a little COMO tradition.

29 S 10th St., (573) 443-5418
harposcomo.com

SLURP UP A CICADA
AT SPARKY'S

Sparky's Homemade Ice Cream is the quintessential mom-and-pop ice cream shop and a Columbia mainstay since 2003. Named after owner Scott Southwick's beloved bulldog, Sparky—whose statue sits outside the store beside his water dish—Sparky's is the place to go for ice cream lovers. Sparky's features over 30 unique flavors, with ingredients sourced from local farms and businesses. They even have a hitching post outside for your four-legged family members. Have an idea for an ice cream flavor? Sparky's takes your requests. Enjoy the eclectic mix of over 100 not-so-great art pieces adorning the walls as well as the stuffed animal fridge. Memorable flavors: Oreo Speedwagon, candied bacon, and cicada ice cream—yep, you read that correctly—flavored with the locust-y bugs that emerge from the ground every decade.

21 S 9th St., (573) 447-7400
sparkyshomemadeicecream.com

PADDLE OVER
TO LOGBOAT

Housed in an old meat-packing plant, Logboat Brewing Company has been a Columbia favorite since 2013 and boasts an impressive menu of brews, ciders, and cocktails. They also distribute their craft beer to 53 counties across the state. The bar and tabletops are built of reconditioned wood from historic Missouri sites, adding a rich, textured vibe to the place. Don't expect any food to be served here; this is a true Taproom. But don't fret—Columbia's best food trucks make appearances Thursday through Saturday. Enjoy the outdoor fenced-in area during the warm weather—throw a blanket on the grass, play cornhole or bocce ball, and take in the live music. Make sure to grab some canned beer on your way out, along with some sweet merch: hoodies, tees, caps, and even a collar for your mutt!

504 Fay St., (573) 397-6786
logboatbrewing.com

FILL YOUR GROWLER
AT FLAT BRANCH

The oldest of the local downtown breweries, Flat Branch Pub and Brewery is a Columbia mainstay. Originally founded in 1994, Flat Branch is housed in a century-old brick warehouse that was once a Hudson automobile dealership. Take your food and drink indoors in the vintage, dark-wood-and-brick environs or enjoy the large, modern, fenced-in patio for a little al fresco dining. Fair warning: the patio fills up quickly when the weather is nice, so get there early. Flat Branch has its own certified master brewer and a wide variety of craft beers with ingredients like honey, corn, herbs, and hops sourced from local farms—and you can even view the massive, stainless steel brewing tanks making the magic happen through glassed-in windows. Couple all that with comfort foods like mac and cheese, burgers, and brick-oven pizza, and Flat Branch hits the spot.

115 S 5th St., (573) 499-0400
flatbranch.com

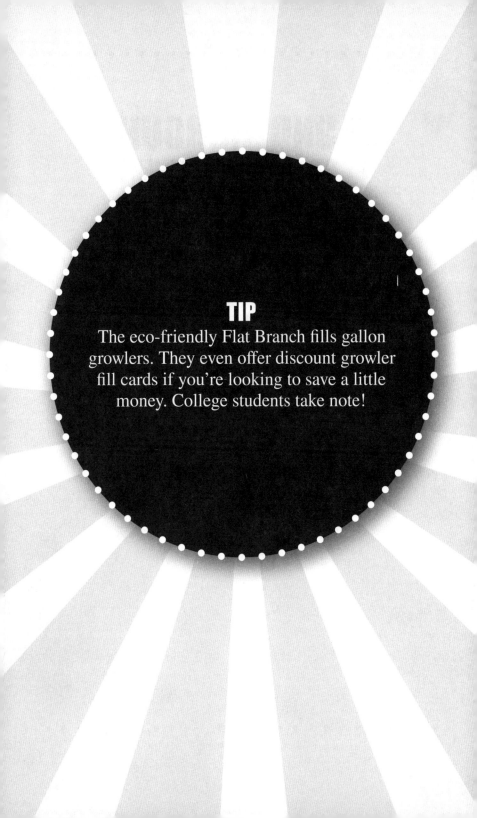

TIP

The eco-friendly Flat Branch fills gallon growlers. They even offer discount growler fill cards if you're looking to save a little money. College students take note!

GO UNDERGROUND
AT BROADWAY BREWERY

Located smack-dab in the heart of downtown, Broadway Brewery is nestled below street level like a secret hideaway. But what makes this restaurant and brewery a local favorite is no mystery. It is one of the premier farm-to-table restaurants in mid-Missouri. Owner Walker Claridge sources locally grown produce, free-range meats, and grass-fed dairy for the brewery's eclectic and distinctly regional menu to ensure a commitment to local farms and access to local foods. But a brewery is about beer, right? Broadway Brewery has an impressive collection of over 30 hand-crafted brews, and you can find their canned stock sold both in the restaurant and throughout Missouri. Come in for the amazing Sunday brunch or the Columbia Jazz Orchestra performing live the last Monday of each month.

816 E Broadway, (573) 443-5054
broadwaybrewery.com

OTHER BREWERIES
SERVING LOCAL CRAFT BEER

1839 Tap House
212 E Green Meadows Rd., Ste. 2, (573) 441-1839
1839taphouse.com

Twain Missouri Taproom
The Tiger Hotel, 23 S 8th St., (573) 875-8888
thetigerhotel.com/experience/twain

The International Taphouse
308 S 9th St., (573) 443-1401
internationaltaphouse.com

Günter Hans European Pub and Café
7 Hitt St., (573) 722-4045
gunterhans.com

9th Street Public House
36 N 9th St., (573) 777-9782
facebook.com/9thstreetpublichouse

BRANCH OUT BEYOND THE BISCUIT
AT OZARK MOUNTAIN

Owner Bryan Maness honors the food traditions that five generations of his Northeast Arkansas family refined in the foothills of the Ozarks—and you can taste it in every bite. Ozark Mountain Biscuit & Bar started out as a food truck known for its homegrown and locally sourced meat and vegetables and made-from-scratch buttermilk biscuit sandwiches. But the brick-and-mortar store has upped its game far beyond the biscuit. You can still savor the mouthwatering bacon, sausage or egg biscuits and gravy along with traditional pulled pork, Cajun catfish, meats, tempeh, and veggies. But now you can enjoy a morning coffee and pastry or savory homestyle sandwiches, soups, and salads. They're good food, plain and simple. When the weather's nice, take it all out onto the spacious outdoor deck and enjoy. Their award-winning food truck rolls into farmers markets and makes regular stops throughout town.

1204 Hinkson Ave., (573) 447-6547
ozarkbiscuits.com

TIP
You can pick up their "Take 'n Bake" biscuits in local grocery stores, such as Hy-Vee, Moser's, Schnucks, Clover's, Eat Well, and the Root Cellar.

GET ECLECTIC
AT FRETBOARD

Located in the North Village Arts District, Fretboard Coffee has a distinct community vibe unmatched in the Columbia coffee scene. Housed in an old garage, Fretboard is part coffee shop, part music venue, and part art gallery. Enjoy a rollicking happy hour Monday through Friday along with local acoustic and jazz musicians and singer-songwriters. First Fridays celebrations also feature pop-up art sales on their outdoor patio. But this is still an award-winning coffee shop, sharing ethically sourced, organically grown coffees from around the world. They're the good guys; they support local causes and focus on sustainability with biodegradable packaging and composting for local farms. If you can't venture downtown, catch their coffee truck at the Columbia Farmers Market and other local events. Love the logo and merch: hats, mugs, snifters, and of course, lots of coffee. Check it all out online!

1013 E Walnut St., #10, (573) 227-2233
fretboardcoffee.com

JUST TRY
JUST JEFF'S

If you're into hefty burgers and Chicago-style dogs, look no further than Just Jeff's. Owner Jeff Spencer started modestly, selling hot dogs from a cart on the Mizzou campus in 2013, but now he has two brick-and-mortar stores and two "Best Burger" awards from *Inside Columbia* magazine. But fair warning: this no-frills burger joint isn't for the faint of heart. You haven't lived until you've sampled their breakfast cheeseburger with a fried egg on top, their mountainous Frito pie—an original twist on nachos—or their bacon dog. Yep, a deep-fried hot dog wrapped in crispy bacon. Your cardiologist doesn't need to know! Just Jeff's is worth a stop and will satisfy all your meaty food cravings. Staffing issues that resulted in temporary store closures in 2021 appear to have been solved, with newly trained teams ready to take on a busy 2022!

701 Business Loop 70 W, (573) 239-6097
510 E Green Meadows St., Ste. 101, (573) 356-1306
ilovejustjeffs.com

GAS UP AND GUZZLE
AT PIERPONT GENERAL STORE

Where can you find farm-fresh eggs, locally sourced fruits and vegetables, farm-raised meats, plus drinks and live music . . . and then top off your gas tank? Pierpont General Store, of course. New owners Jed and Brandy Taylor performed a bold renovation in 2020, adding an outdoor deck, picnic table seating, and a stage for live music. The new Pierpont Café and Bar's kitchen serves comfort food staples like dogs and brats, biscuits and gravy, grilled cheese, and even Shakespeare's Pizza, while the local Bur Oak and Logboat breweries supply the draft beer. This little gem off the beaten track rocks on the weekends and serves up a not-to-be-missed Sunday brunch. The Pierpont General Store is a must-stop for grub, grog, or gas . . . and probably anything else you can think of.

7650 MO-163, (573) 442-2701
facebook.com/pierpontgeneralstore

TIP
The outdoor seating in the Café and Bar remains open into late fall. A roaring firepit out back helps keep the autumn chill at bay if you can luck into a seat close enough.

CHASE DOWN
LILLY'S CANTINA

Lilly's colorful, flowered food truck, with its palm trees and fronds idling at the curb, is almost enough to make your mouth water. But just wait until you taste their gourmet street food. Lilly's has won the hearts and stomachs of Columbia foodies and is a regular contender for *Inside Columbia* magazine's "Best Food Truck" award. With a signature Baja-Midwest flair to their made-to-order tacos, burritos, quesadillas, and nachos, Lilly's simply can't be beat. As the season changes, so does the menu, but you can always tackle their amazing two-pound, belly-filling burritos. It's not often that a food truck offers lobster and Mahi Mahi, but Lilly's isn't your typical food truck. You can even add a Thai "zing" to your chicken and carnitas, and just about every meal has a veggie option for non-carnivores.

711 Vandiver Dr., Ste. K, (573) 355-4831
lillyscantina.com

SHOP LOCAL
AT COLUMBIA FARMERS MARKET

Located at the MU Healthcare Pavilion in Columbia Agriculture Park, the Columbia Farmers Market is one-stop shopping for local, healthy eating. The year-round, covered facility regularly draws over 4,000 eager weekend shoppers and supports more than 80 local vendors. You can't help but run into someone you know, either buying or selling the amazing farm-to-table produce. Sample the freshest eggs, fruits and veggies, meats, baked goods, gourmet coffee, honey—and my favorite, succulent honeycomb! Drop the kids at the one-room schoolhouse for scavenger hunts, taste tests, arts and crafts, and story time while you hunt and gather. The Park also boasts an interactive urban farm, an outdoor nature playground, and recreational trail. SNAP and WIC benefits are exchangeable for tokens so that all community members have access to locally sourced, healthy fare.

1701 W Ash St., (573) 823-6889
Open year-round on Tuesdays, Thursdays, and Saturdays.
columbiafarmersmarket.org

OTHER COLUMBIA FARMERS MARKETS

Orr Street Farmers and Artisans Market in Wabash Station 126 N 10th St., (573) 239-8874 Open Sundays 9 a.m. to 1 p.m. (April 17–October 30) facebook.com/farmandart	Boone County Farmers Market in Columbia Mall Parking Lot 2300 Bernadette Dr., (573) 817-1367 Open Saturdays 8 a.m. to 12 p.m. (May 1–October 30) boonecountyfarmers.com

SATISFY YOUR SWEET TOOTH
AT THE CANDY FACTORY

For over 40 years, the chocolate connoisseurs at the Candy Factory have been creating the most delectable chocolates, truffles, caramels, cookies, and candies in mid-Missouri. Wonder how it's done? Well, you don't need to be Charlie Bucket or hold a golden ticket to glimpse the magic. Just slip past the counter, walk up the back stairs, and sneak a peek through the factory window as the Oompa Loompas create their world-class confections. Have an idea for a unique creation? The Candy Factory takes requests, making custom confections to your specifications. Enjoy their seasonal specials, and for that birthday, anniversary, or graduation, you can't go wrong with their amazing gift baskets—a relationship saver for countless Columbians! Those worshiping at the low-carb altar should make sure to try their sugar-free collection.

701 Cherry St., (573) 443-8222
thecandyfactoryonline.com

GET A JOLT
AT COFFEE ZONE

Home of the local favorite, Rocket Fuel Blend, Coffee Zone is another tried-and-true java mainstay, having served the downtown area since 1994. Coffee Zone has a diverse offering of signature single-origin and blended coffees and numerous espresso and specialty drinks, as well as traditional Turkish coffee, hot chocolate, and cider. The Zone is known for its outstanding food, and their Mediterranean fare might be the best in town. Don't miss their gyros piled high with meat and veggies, falafel, omelet wraps, labani, and Greek salads. And finish it off with a mouthwatering baklava, cheesecake, or scone. The Mediterranean-themed store has a warm and welcoming atmosphere, and every patron is always greeted with a "hala hala" when they enter, which means hello, goodbye, and thank you all in one!

11 N 9th St., (573) 449-8215
coffeezoneonline.com

DITCH THE MEAT
AT GINA'S

A newcomer to the food truck biz, Gina's Vegan A Go-Go is notable as the only exclusively vegan wagon in mid-Missouri. Billed as vegan comfort food, Gina's delicacies are made from scratch with the goal of sustainability and helping people along in their vegan journey . . . and maybe fooling some carnivores along the way. Are you a vegan newbie? Gina can whip up a hearty meal that tastes like the non-vegan original, and she invites her customers to test her skills! Don't miss the amazing breakfast menu featuring biscuits and vegan-sausage gravy burritos, tofu scramble, and Mexican burritos with vegan chorizo. You'll find plenty of vegan "meats," including burgers, BBQ, and even tuna salad, made with chickpeas and seaweed for that oceany flavor. If you like good food, stop at Gina's and give it a go-go . . . you won't regret it!

609 N Garth Ave.
ginas-vegan-a-go-go.business.site

GRAB A GOULASH
AT CAFÉ POLAND

Owner Robert Galijska opened Café Poland in 2013, but it's his mother, Iwona, who runs the show. She creates the "from-scratch" homemade pierogis, goulash, golbaki, and borscht for the small but mighty army of loyal patrons she serves daily. If you love authentic Polish fare with lots of potatoes, cabbage, stews, and soups, you're in for a treat. Stop in for lunch and you might catch an *I Love Lucy* rerun on the TV or hear symphony music playing on Iwona's record player. The place is cramped but intimate, sparse but warm, with comfort food that will leave you homesick for your mom's cooking. If you're looking for something unique, Café Poland is a mid-Missouri diamond in the rough.

807 Locust St., (573) 874-8929

GET YOUR WINE ON WITH A VIEW
AT LES BOURGEOIS

Les Bourgeois Vineyards has been a premier destination spot for wine, friends, and food since 1974. Overlooking the scenic Missouri River, this gem has a little something for everyone. Looking to sample some meats, cheeses, or gourmet chocolate curated to complement an award-winning wine while soaking up the sun? The outdoor A-frame wine garden is the place for you. In search of casual dining with spectacular views? Head inside to the Bistro. There's also a wine-tasting room and gift shop. Les Bourgeois also features a great lineup of events throughout the year. Itching to strip off those socks and stomp grapes in a barrel? Of course, you are! Then don't miss the Crush Festival each September. There's also an annual summer music event, winery tour, blufftop yoga (with wine, naturally), the Rocheport Wine Stroll, and more.

14020 W Hwy. BB, Rocheport, MO
A-Frame: (573) 698-3401
Blufftop Bistro: (573) 698-2300
Tasting Room: (573) 698-2716
missouriwine.com

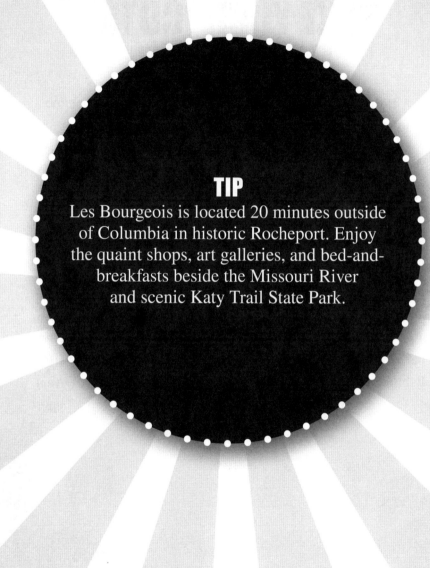

TIP

Les Bourgeois is located 20 minutes outside of Columbia in historic Rocheport. Enjoy the quaint shops, art galleries, and bed-and-breakfasts beside the Missouri River and scenic Katy Trail State Park.

TAKE YOUR "CUTS"
AT THE BARRED OWL

The Barred Owl Butcher & Table isn't just another Columbia farm-to-table restaurant. It's also an artisan butcher shop and "old world" delicatessen focusing on the art of charcuterie. The restaurant sources seasonally available Missouri produce from local farms, so the menu is always fresh and innovative. Their whole-animal philosophy dictates that what's not used in the restaurant is salvaged—smoked or cured into hand-crafted cuts. But ethical and responsible sourcing aside, the Barred Owl is simply a great place to eat! Owners Joshua Smith and Ben Parks's diverse culinary backgrounds complement each other perfectly—think traditional Midwest with a New Orleans flare. The wait staff are also skilled and knowledgeable. The vibrant restaurant has a bustling warehouse-y vibe, with vintage Edison lighting and an open kitchen that lends to the lively ambience.

47 E Broadway, (573) 442-9323
barredowlbutcher.com

TIP

The Barred Owl is only open for dinner Wednesday through Saturday (4:30 p.m. to close) and Sunday brunch (10:30 a.m. to 2 p.m.). But the butcher shop is open Wednesday through Saturday (1 p.m. to 6 p.m.), so you can still get your favorite cuts even when the restaurant isn't serving.

MEET A FRIEND
AT LAKOTA

Established in 1992, Lakota Coffee has stood the test of time. The word *Lakota* originates from the Teton Sioux and means "friendly people," which is what you'll find here. Lakota is warm and welcoming, with beautiful handmade hickory tables and Native American tapestries decorating the 1920s-era brick walls. They source their single-origin beans from some of the highest elevations in the world and slow roast them on-site in a monster San Franciscan Roaster that will grab your attention. The menu offers numerous lattes, mochas, shakes, frappes, and smoothies as well as panini sandwiches and mouthwatering pastries and snacks. Lakota clientele are a perfect snapshot of the Columbia community: students, shoppers, local businesspeople, and professionals—and Lakota honors that community by supporting many local charities as well as a number of Native American causes.

4 S 9th St., (573) 874-2825
311 Green Meadows Way, (573) 499-9901
1 Hospital Dr., (573) 884-4766
(Coffee Kiosk in the University of Missouri Hospital)
lakotacoffee.com

GET UP
ON THE ROOF

Looking for great food and cocktails? How about the best view of downtown Columbia? Then climb to the top of the Broadway Columbia Hotel. Open since 2014, The Roof is 112 feet from the ground and provides breathtaking, panoramic city views. The Roof offers open-air seating throughout the year with a full-service bar, two firepits on the east and west ends, and a top-notch menu offering sandwiches, small plate meals, cocktails, wine, beer, and local hand-crafted brews from Logboat and Bur Oak breweries. Live local music and DJ-spun favorites will keep you dancing 'til late. Guys, you'll need to shed those t-shirts and flip flops to meet the dress code, but you'll be glad you did. The Roof's New Year's Eve event is one you don't want to miss. And don't forget to reserve your custom, heated igloo—with your own dedicated server!

1111 E Broadway, (573) 875-7000
thebroadwaycolumbia.com/the-roof

JOIN THE CLUB
AT PERCHE CREEK

Perche Creek Café serves genuine down-home breakfast and lunch, and with a local flavor that isn't limited to the menu. Sure, their biscuits and gravy, pancakes, and omelets are some of the best you'll find—and their pork tenderloin sandwich is the stuff of legend—but the Café's atmosphere is what sets it apart. From the local patrons and servers' friendly banter to the décor, the atmosphere is firmly tongue in cheek—and not for cleaning food scraps from behind the teeth. Case in point: the Café's Perche Creek Yacht Club. With no body of water or yachts to speak of, the Club has 1,000 members worldwide who meet regularly to "further its mission of having no purpose." Don't miss their annual Cow Patty Bingo fundraiser to support the Central Missouri Food Bank.

6751 US Hwy. 40, (573) 446-7400
perchecreekcafe.wordpress.com/our-menu

TIP

If you haven't experienced Cow Patty Bingo yet, put it on your to-do list. If you're confused, here's a quick rule summary: Borrow a cow. Place numbered placards on ground in grassy field. Let cow roam field after eating. Remain patient. Closest placard wins. Does that help?

PULL UP
TO MUGS UP

The last of a 60-store chain launched in the 1950s, Mugs Up is a classic and authentic drive-in restaurant. Carhops take your order and even balance your food on window trays like they did during the decade of Elvis and Little Richard. Truth be told, Mugs Up hasn't changed much since Ray Kewley opened the store in 1955. The Kewley family still runs it. The building and the recipes are pretty much the same—burgers, dogs, and chili served in various combinations along with cherry cokes and root beer floats. Fries were added to the menu in the 1980s, but if you want ice cream in a cup, there's still only vanilla. Mugs Up is so old-school they don't take credit cards and they don't advertise. So, bring your cash or checkbook, and make sure to spread the word to keep this place alive for the next generation!

603 Orange St., (573) 442-9833
facebook.com/mugsupdrivein

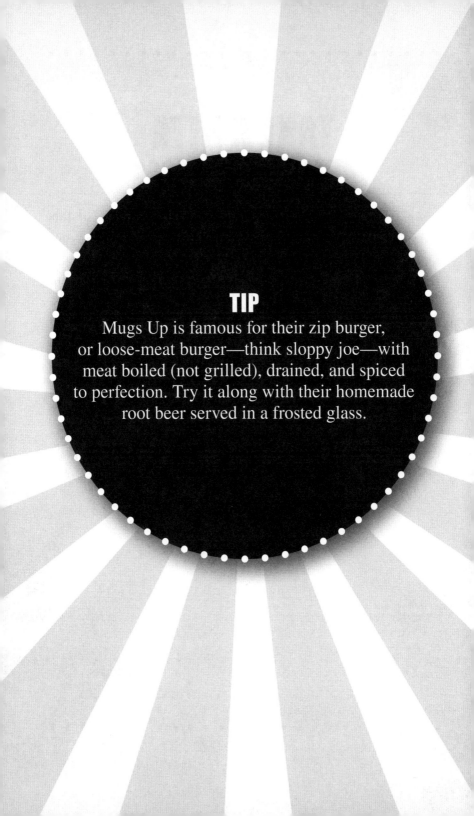

TIP

Mugs Up is famous for their zip burger, or loose-meat burger—think sloppy joe—with meat boiled (not grilled), drained, and spiced to perfection. Try it along with their homemade root beer served in a frosted glass.

TAKE A BITE
AT THE GATOR WAGON

If you're looking for Columbia unique, you've found it with this Evergladian food truck! Bayou fare might not be on everyone's radar, but it will be after you sample Gator Wagon's real gator, fried up golden brown and served on tacos and other mouth-watering platters. Be adventurous and try the gator bites, a gator sub, or the swamp platter with gator, catfish, and hushpuppies. Other Cajun favorites like frog legs, Cajun tacos, and fish filets will hit the spot. The loaded potachos—kettle fried potato chips piled high with meat, cheese, jalapenos, and sour cream—are a unique riff on traditional nachos and worth the gamble. For the timid or squeamish, you can't beat their loaded hot dogs. Don't be ashamed—you can always tell everyone it's a gator dog . . .

(573) 220-1555
facebook.com/gatorwagon

CELEBRATE THE ISLANDS
AT THE JERK HUT

Chalk up 20 years of mid-Missouri success to authentic, sizzling Jamaican fare that will satisfy belly and soul as it transports you to the tropics. The Jamaican Jerk Hut isn't fancy, but it features the islands' "street food" that owners Rex Scott and Colin Russell were weaned on—a tantalizing, sweet-and-smoky jerk chicken as well as wings, pork, beef patties, and curry chicken, marinated in a 48-hour soak of tropical island spices and grilled to perfection. For the adventurous, take a chance on some oxtail or goat. Finish it off with a feisty, tropical Rasta Lemonade made with mammea apples imported from the islands or a Jamaican soda. Their mobile eatery preceded their brick-and-mortar shack and landed them a spot on *Inside Columbia* magazine's "Best Food Truck" category.

711 Vandiver Dr., (573) 607-9779
jamaican-jerk-hut.business.site

TIP
If you haven't ever seen the Jamaican Jerk Hut's food truck, search for it live or online. Their irreverent tag line is one I can't reveal here, but it will have you in stitches.

LOAD UP
AT LEE STREET

Located in a house basement off Mizzou's east campus, the Lee Street Deli (LSD) has been serving neighborhood residents for over 90 years. What started as a corner grocery store in 1927 evolved into a takeout deli and eatery. In 2015, owners Nicole and Will Muirhead bought the LSD—and yes, the owners play up the psychedelic reference—added a grill, obtained a liquor license, expanded business hours, and included in-seat dining. They offer lots of great comfort food, but try their magic CBR (chicken, bacon, ranch), signature Juicy Burger (loose meat sandwich), or the Frito pie in a bag . . . don't ask, just get it! The LSD also remains close to their grocery store roots, selling convenience items like deodorant, paper towels, and toothpaste, as well as beer, cocktails, shots, 12-packs, and hard seltzers to go, Juul and tobacco products . . . even ping-pong balls.

603 Lee St., (573) 442-4111
eatlsd.com

TAKE YOUR LICKS
AT BUCK'S

Buck's Ice Cream is legendary in Columbia for one reason: Tiger Stripe ice cream. Since 1992, the black and gold, creamy favorite has captured the hearts and stomachs of Mizzou fans and remains a tradition at university and alumni events. But making ice cream with the Mizzou colors and realistic tiger stripes wasn't a walk—or prowl—in the park. It took Mizzou's extensive 100-year history of ice cream research to come up with an edible, gold-colored French vanilla and Dutch dark chocolate mixed at proper ratios. Buck's is located in Eckles Hall on the Mizzou campus, and the food science students there experiment with new concoctions regularly, but they always have their traditional flavors on hand: vanilla, chocolate, cookies and cream, rocky road, butter pecan, and black walnut.

1406 E Rollins St., (573) 882-1088
cafnr.missouri.edu/bucks-ice-cream

TIP

Ice cream research at Mizzou goes back to 1929, but it took 60 years before someone came up with a Black & Gold flavor. One of their first efforts at a palatable Tiger Stripe Ice Cream was a visually appealing—but awful tasting—licorice and orange sherbet mix. Good thing they didn't stop there!

CHOW DOWN
AT BIG DADDY'S

Big Daddy's BBQ is a comfort food mecca! Owners Ernie and Fontella Lloyd come from a long line of barbecue restauranteurs who know the secret is in the sauce. Their Kansas City–style barbecue features pulled pork, riblets, brisket and ribs, pork steaks, Polish sausage, and smoked chicken wings that will melt in your mouth and stick to your ribs. The meat is served with generous sides of baked beans, collard greens, potato salad, and slaw, so you'll never leave hungry! Their pork nachos are an instant favorite, a virtual mountain of pulled pork, baked beans, jalapenos, cheese, and barbecue sauce over chips! If somehow you can't find these pitmasters' bright red BBQ shack near the business loop, you're bound to see one of their two food trucks serving up their "meats on the streets" somewhere close.

1205 N Garth Ave., (573) 875-2227
facebook.com/bigdaddysbbqcomo

GO LOCAL
AT CAFÉ BERLIN

When your head chef describes cooking as a "collaboration between heart and desire," you know the food will be special. And at Café Berlin, it is. The place is known for its creative menu filled with organic grains, beans, and flour, and locally sourced meats and produce. It's the go-to site for the vegetarians, vegans, and gluten-frees wandering among us. But don't panic, carnivores—you have plenty of pork and beef dishes to choose from. Café Berlin has also teamed with Fretboard Coffee on a custom blend to fill the eclectic coffee mugs the café is famous for. The weekend brunch lines are lengthy, so get there early— and don't even think of calling ahead, because they don't do reservations. Tired of battling the crowds? Save time and hit up the new to-go kitchen.

220 N 10th St., (573) 441-0400
cafeberlincomo.com

MUSIC
AND ENTERTAINMENT

DIG THE RIFFS
AT ROOTS 'N BLUES

Looking for live music, arts and crafts vendors, great food and drink, and maybe even a 5K, 10K, or half-marathon? You've found it at the Roots 'N Blues Music Festival. This annual, three-day shindig held at Stephens Lake Park reads like a who's who of blues, gospel, bluegrass, folk, country, rock, and soul music. Past headliners Buddy Guy; Gary Clark, Jr.; The Avett Brothers; Al Green; Ben Harper; Brandi Carlile; and Sheryl Crow only scratch the surface of the amazing talent the event draws. The festival does a lot of things right: plenty of food options, 'green' vendors who provide recycling incentives; and cashless RFID wristbands that speed the concession lines. Roots 'N Blues is an all-day event, so bring lawn chairs or a blanket to throw on the grass. Now in its 16th year, Roots 'N Blues is one of Columbia's signature events that you don't want to miss!

Stephens Lake Park
2001 E Broadway
rootsnbluesfestival.com

TIP

Roots 'N Blues has no parking on-site. Free shuttles run to and from downtown Columbia to the festival gates. Children are welcome at the event, and with your wristbands you can come and go as you please.

GATHER BESIDE
THE BIG MUDDY

There is a bend on the Missouri River that surveyor Ira P. Nash once called "the most beautiful spot in all creation." Home to Cooper's Landing since 1989, the "bend" has always been a place to gather with friends, share a beer, and celebrate live music. But after a major flood in 2019, owner Richard King had an opportunity to reimagine the site. Today, tent and RV camping are available, along with laundry and shower facilities, a general store, food trucks, and of course, live music and beer. Cooper's Landing is the only full-service marina on the Big Muddy between St. Louis and Kansas City and even offers motorboat excursions from April to August. Situated on the Katy Trail—and with access to state parks, hunting, and conservation areas—Cooper's Landing is the perfect spot to pick your passion.

11505 Smith Hatchery Rd., (573) 657-1299
cooperslandingmo.com

CATCH A FLICK
AT TRUE/FALSE

Another of Columbia's signature events, the True/False Film Fest (T/F), is an internationally acclaimed, four-day documentary film festival held each March. It started modestly, with just 4,000 tickets sold in its inaugural year. That number has ballooned to over 54,000, attracting filmgoers from around the world. It takes a village to raise a film festival, and the city has rallied around this shared community experience for 18 years. Films are screened at eight different downtown venues, from local cinemas and theaters to music halls, university auditoriums, hotels, and churches. T/F also showcases Columbia's best restaurants and features music and concerts, art, late night parties, and Q&As with visiting filmmakers. With so many transformative films featured each year, T/F has become a beloved annual downtown tradition. And don't miss the kickoff parade, the March March, a colorful display of art, noise, costume, and music all rolled into one.

T/F Fest Office, (573) 442-8783
truefalse.org

TIP

T/F has several levels of participation, and it can get pricey for those who want access to every film, event, and late-night party. Just interested in films? Go with the $105 Simple Pass. It provides 10 reserved tickets in advance. But even if you can't reserve a must-see film on your list, you can line up for any film via "the Q" and you'll most likely get in—if you get there early!

DAB A BRUSH, DRINK A BLUSH
AT THE CANVAS ON BROADWAY

Remember how much fun you had back in fourth grade art class? Grabbing a paintbrush and slinging half the paint onto a canvas and the other half onto your smock? Well, fast-forward 20 years, add some wine, and you have The Canvas on Broadway. They even provide the smocks! The Canvas on Broadway offers expert guidance recreating one of their more than 100 sample paintings, complete with music and alcohol to keep the evening interesting. It's great for large groups or a night out on the town. The Canvas has classes for children and families, too, including birthday parties. They also host private events. The two-and-a-half-hour classes are a decent bang for the buck, considering the art instruction and the 16″x20″ finished canvas you get to take home.

706 E Broadway, Ste. 100, (573) 443-2222
thecanvasonbroadway.com

RESURRECT THE PAST
AT THE HERITAGE FESTIVAL

The annual Heritage Festival and Craft Show is a celebratory glimpse into America's history. The 43-year-old festival features re-enactors, artisans, and tradespersons from across the state in traditional 19th-century regalia selling hand-crafted merch and demonstrating "lost" trades. Three stages showcase live Celtic, Cajun, blues, folk, western, and bluegrass music as well as craft shows, cultural performers, magicians, puppet shows, and traditional storytellers—including Saturday evening ghost stories! Hayrides, crafts, and games will keep the little ones entertained. Tour the three historic houses to get the authentic flavor of 19th-century life. Food trucks and festival fare enrich the experience. Many of the vendors are cash-only, so hit the ATM before you get there. The two-day festival is not only a wonderful educational experience, but a lively weekend of fun, food, and entertainment.

Historic Nifong Park
3700 Ponderosa St., (573) 874-6341
como.gov/parks-and-recreation/special-events-2/
annual-heritage-festival-craft-show

TIP
Parking at the Heritage Festival can be a challenge. However, free shuttle buses are available at Discovery Office Park (just up the road) and run round trip throughout the festival.

A-MAZE YOURSELF
AT SHRYOCK'S FARMS

There aren't enough superlatives to describe Shryock's Callaway Farms's annual themed 16-acre towering corn maze. High-tech computer programs create their unique, artistic designs and GPS technology brings it to life—but you don't have to understand it to enjoy it. Just slip into the corn and solve the clues at different checkpoints to help find the way out. And don't panic! Marked exits come to the rescue if you get lost. You can also enjoy the farm's hayrides and massive jumping pillow or gather with friends around the campfire. Finish off with a visit to the Big Red Barn and sample their tasty hot chocolate and cider, or grab a caramel apple, kettle corn, or some ice cream. For 25 cents, send a gumball through the tracks, slots, and gadgets of the three-story gumball coaster. Whatever you choose, Shryock's is the perfect way to spend a crisp fall afternoon.

2927 County Rd. 253, (573) 592-0191
callawayfarms.com

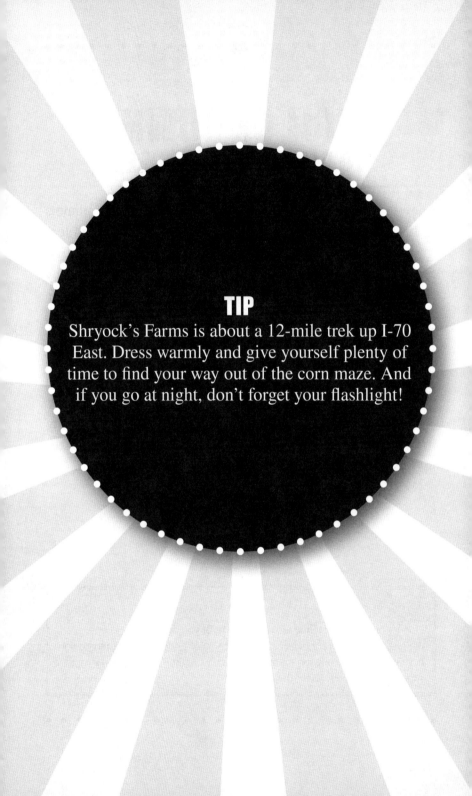

TIP

Shryock's Farms is about a 12-mile trek up I-70 East. Dress warmly and give yourself plenty of time to find your way out of the corn maze. And if you go at night, don't forget your flashlight!

ROLL ON DOWN
TO PEDALER'S JAMBOREE

Looking for an 80-mile round-trip bike ride from Columbia to Jefferson City with music and libations along the way? Join a cast of characters for Pedaler's Jamboree, a weekend party/music festival on wheels along the scenic Katy Trail. Enjoy breathtaking views of the Missouri River as you visit trailside venues in McBaine, Cooper's Landing, and Hartsburg serving up live music, food, and beverages. But be warned, pace yourself with the latter—you have a lot of miles to pedal! The trail ends at Ellis-Porter Park in Jefferson City for the main stage concerts that go late into Saturday night. You can camp overnight or pamper yourself in a city hotel. On Sunday, you backtrack along the trail and do it all over again. Make sure to rally for the late-night Sunday after-party at Rose Music Hall.

pedalersjamboree.com

TIP

Don't worry about hauling all your stuff with you on the ride. The organizers deliver your bags each way. If you're falling behind (maybe you have a flat) or had one too many at Cooper's Landing, they provide "sag" support and deliver you to the next stop.

CARVE OUT SOME PUMPKIN TIME
IN HARTSBURG

The charming river town of Hartsburg has some of the most fertile farmland in Missouri, and they showcase it each year with the Hartsburg Pumpkin Festival. Each October, the self-proclaimed "Missouri's Pumpkin Patch" is transformed into the most popular spot in Boone County. What's truly amazing is that a town of 105 pulls off this two-day festival for thousands of visitors. There are hundreds of arts/crafts and food vendors, bounce houses, petting zoos, pony rides, and live music played from the town's gazebo. And, of course, pumpkins—tens of thousands of them—grown on Hartsburg farms. Don't miss the pumpkin carving/painting and pie eating contests. The Hartsburg Pumpkin Festival is a little slice of Americana less than 20 miles from Columbia—a short trip for a lasting memory.

Hartsburg, MO, (573) 808-1288
hartsburgpumpkinfest.com

TIP
The line of cars jostling their way into Hartsburg on Festival days is epic. If you want to avoid sitting in traffic, stay away from Route A, the main road into town. Google "E Christian School Rd." That will take you the back way and save you an hour. You could also bicycle along the Katy Trail into Hartsburg. Of course, it may be a difficult ride back carrying a pumpkin!

CRACK THE BINDING
AT UNBOUND

The Unbound Book Festival draws award-winning national and international writers and poets to Columbia each spring to help inspire a lifelong love of the written word. The one-of-a-kind event is the brainchild of novelist Alex George, owner of downtown's Skylark Bookshop. Relocated from Stephens College to downtown in 2022, Unbound features author panels and Q&As, children's events, poetry readings, writing workshops, jazz music, and book signings, among other entertainment. Local independent authors also have a forum to display and sell their work. Unbound's greatest gift may be the Authors in the Schools program they've developed to inspire the community's next generation of writers. Going strong for seven years now, the Unbound Book Festival is 100 percent volunteer-run and free to the public! Take advantage of one of the city's great cultural events.

608 Westmount Ave.
unboundbookfestival.com

CATCH AN INDIE
AT RAGTAG

Dinner, drinks, and a movie? Get them all at Ragtag Cinema, where strong lineups of ambitious films are always on the menu. The idea was hatched in 1998, when a "rag tag" group of film lovers began screening independent films downtown. Then they partnered with some pals who owned a bar and bakery, and the Ragtag Cinemacafé was born. Today, it's just the Ragtag Cinema, and while they've gone high-tech with 35mm and digital projectors in two large-screen theaters, there's still an eclectic spirit to the operation. Where else can you watch films on a sofa with a beer in hand and leave with soup, a sandwich, and a loaf of artisan bread? A staunch supporter of the arts, Ragtag has been a primary venue of the True/False Film Fest since 2004.

10 Hitt St., (573) 441-8504
ragtagcinema.org

TIP

The Ragtag Cinema and True/False Film Fest are intricately intertwined. The group that founded Ragtag Cinema includes Paul Sturtz and David Wilson, who launched T/F in 2004 and built it into an internationally acclaimed film festival.

WATCH A FLICK IN THE PARK
AT COSMO PARK

The aroma of buttery-fresh popcorn wafting from an old-fashioned trolley cart . . . families lounging on blankets and lawn chairs . . . kids running through a grass field with snow cones dripping from their hands. Picturing something from a Norman Rockwell painting? Well, Movies in the Park at Cosmo Park comes as close to capturing that sense of small-town charm and community as anything you can imagine. From June through September, Columbia hosts a summer lineup of favorite family-friendly movies shared beneath the stars. It may be the best distraction-free family time you'll spend this year—unless you consider running into old friends and neighbors a distraction. And the best part about it, it's free! Bring a blanket to throw on the grass and a couple of lawn chairs, and you're all set. One of Columbia's best family events made better by familiar faces and Columbia's great lineup of food trucks!

Cosmo Park
1650 Business Loop 70 W, (573) 874-7460
como.gov/parks-and-recreation/special-events-2/movies-in-the-park

EXPERIENCE
THE MISSOURI CONTEMPORARY BALLET

Since 2006, the Missouri Contemporary Ballet has been fulfilling its mission to transform lives through dance—but they're definitely not your father's ballet! They boast over 60 original productions that are bold and edgy, with high-energy, athletic performances. The company's reputation extends to both national and international audiences, but their loyalty is clearly to their mid-Missouri community. The Ballet's outreach to local schools, assisted-living facilities, and those with special needs and differing abilities, along with its provision of dance scholarships for youth in need, have only cemented that commitment. You can catch the company in full swing at the University Concert Series performances at the Missouri Theatre. Or if you're looking for a swinging night on the town, enjoy the mega-popular annual fundraising event, "Dancing with the Missouri Stars!"

110 Orr St., Ste. 102, (573) 219-7134
missouricontemporaryballet.org

TIP

After a three-year COVID-19–related hiatus, "Dancing with the Missouri Stars!" is back in 2022. The event features eight local celebrities (from the community), each paired with a Missouri Contemporary Ballet dancer. Supporting a celebrity with a donation directly supports the Ballet.

MOSEY ON DOWN
TO THE MOSY

The Missouri Symphony (MOSY) has been entertaining, inspiring, and educating mid-Missourians for over 50 years. The MOSY conservatory supports the musical education of children with their youth orchestra and symphony, chamber music initiative, and music skills and knowledge courses. They provide apprenticeship programs, musical competitions, and even cash awards to support emerging and exceptional young musical artists. MOSY also collaborates with the Missouri Contemporary Ballet each year in an immersive performance of two classical art forms in support of both organizations' missions. In the winter, you can catch the MOSY during its Holiday Home Tour and annual fundraiser, Symphony of Toys. During the warmer months, don't miss the six-week music festival, "Hot Summer Nights," and sample a range of musical expressions to satisfy all tastes.

203 S 9th St., (573) 875-0600
themosy.org

ROCK THE HOUSE
AT THE BLUE NOTE

Every town needs a place where the best bands come to play, and in Columbia that place is the Blue Note. Owners Matt Gerding and Scott Leslie are continuing the legacy of Richard King, who established the Blue Note in 1980. Since that time, some of the greatest names in music have rocked the historic,100-year-old theater on their way through town: REM, the Pixies, Chuck Berry, Wilco, Ryan Adams, the Dave Matthews Band, Willie Nelson, and Red Hot Chili Peppers, just to name a few. With an upper balcony, opera box seats, and proscenium arch above the stage, the revamped theater maintains its elegant pedigree but with a rock 'n roll edge to it. Don't miss the Summerfest series, where live acts rock the downtown streets from April to September.

17 9th St., (573) 874-1944
thebluenote.com

TAKE IN A SHOW
AT THE MISSOURI THEATRE

It's easy to get sidetracked at the Missouri Theatre. The Belgian marble, gilded balconies, stained glass panels, and opulent Italian, crystal chandelier quickly become the main attraction. Just stepping into the lobby transports you back to the roaring '20s! Modeled after the Paris Opera House, the Missouri Theatre is the only pre-talkies movie theater and vaudeville stage in mid-Missouri. Listed on the National Registry of Historic Places, the theatre even has the original organ used for silent-film sound effects. Currently owned and operated by the University of Missouri, the venue is regularly used for stage shows, comedy, concerts, symphonies, and ballet, and it also serves as a screening venue for the True/False Film Festival. A visit to the Missouri Theatre is a Columbia must . . . but try to pay attention to the show!

203 S 9th St., (573) 883-3781
concertseries.missouri.edu/venue/missouri-theatre

EMBRACE THE BARNIES
AT MAPLEWOOD BARN THEATER

Looking for rollicking summer entertainment? You can't beat the Maplewood Barn Theater, which has been providing live, high-quality community theater since 1973. Enjoy a picnic basket and bottle of wine on a blanket beneath the stars as you witness the "Barnies" ply their craft. The theater produces up to five programs from April to October and switches to radio theater during the offseason. The theater also supports the arts, awarding scholarships to promising local high school thespians. In 2010, fire destroyed the 133-year-old barn, sets, and costumes, but the community rallied with donations and labor to help the theater rebuild, reboot, and rise from the ashes. Don't miss this amazing showcase for local talent, with every production a must-see attraction.

2900 E Nifong Blvd., (573) 227-2276
maplewoodbarn.com

WATCH THE WINDOWS
COME TO LIFE DOWNTOWN

On the first Friday of December, the Living Windows Festival kicks off the downtown holiday celebrations. The streets fill up as downtown shopkeepers replace storefront window displays with live performance art, such as cookie baking, storytelling, dancing, or acting out holiday scenes. And while you peer through the glass, strolling carolers pass by singing holiday tunes, a "magic" tree burns brightly on the corner of 9th and Broadway, projected snowflakes fall from building walls, and selfie stations provide festive photo ops with the family! The streets are packed, and stores stay open late hosting open houses. You might even catch a Santa or two making a downtown appearance. A great family event, this unique celebration highlights the creativity and cheer of the community and propels you headlong into the holidays!

visitcolumbiamo.com/directory/living-windows-festival

PUT SOME MAGIC IN YOUR HOLIDAY
AT CHERRY HILL

Close your eyes and picture a huge cherry tree with every inch of its trunk and branches wrapped in thousands of holiday lights. Now imagine the multi-colored, mosaic light pattern framed against the night sky. You've got the Magic Tree, a sight that attracts visitors from across the state in droves throughout the holidays. It's the brainchild of a mystery man known as Will Treelighter—the legend goes—who would wrap his front yard tree in holiday lights each year. The spectacle grew into a motorized holiday pilgrimage—and nightly neighborhood traffic jams—as people descended on his home for a peek. Today, Treelighter plies his craft in the Village of Cherry Hill, the designated spot for holiday revelers seeking to share the holiday spirit. So, bundle up and experience the magic.

210 Cherry Hill Dr.
magic-tree.org

TIP
If you can't make it to Cherry Hill, a second and third Magic Tree are lit at the Unity Center on Broadway and at the Crossing Church on Grindstone Parkway; the latter is not a Will Treelighter project.

SAMPLE THE SWEET CANDY CANE CRIB
AT LOGBOAT

This 300,000-holiday-light display began at Ryan Schultz's home over 10 years ago. He created a modest—well, not so modest, more like over the top—neighborhood holiday-light extravaganza. A victim of his own success, Schultz relocated the ever-expanding Candy Cane Crib to Logboat Brewing Company's property to spread the holiday cheer to greater numbers. The Crib faced a crisis in 2020 when holiday grinches made off with Schultz's trailer filled with $15,000 worth of lights, cords, and gear. But Columbia rallied, donations poured in, and local businesses stepped up and made it possible for this holiday tradition to continue. The lighting ceremony just before Thanksgiving is a must, with holiday movies shown on the outdoor big screen, food trucks, craft beer, and more!

504 Fay St., (573) 489-2123
facebook.com/candycanecrib

CATCH THE HOLIDAY SPIRIT ... DRIVE-THRU STYLE
AT VETERANS UNITED

If you're one of those people who frequents a local drive-thru or two—and who doesn't?—then we've got the holiday light display for you. Take a spin over to the Bright Lights Holiday Nights, a one-mile loop of lights, displays, and music at the Veterans United Home Loan headquarters. Now in its second year, the display features an animated drive-thru tunnel, a 3D starburst, a polygon tree, and several walk-through (or sit-in) cupcakes and ornaments. You can't get out of your vehicle, so plan to hoof it if you want to take advantage of the walk-throughs. The most "corporate" of the local displays, Bright Lights is still a perfect accompaniment to those annual trips through local neighborhoods in search of that "drive-thru" holiday spirit.

4700 S Providence Rd.

TIP

The display is open to the public December 7 through 20, 6:30 p.m. to 10 p.m. The traffic lines tend to be long, so give yourself plenty of time—and lay off the horn, it's the holidays!

PICK A PUMPKIN
AT PEACH TREE

Located just up I-70 West in Booneville, Peach Tree Farms has become a fall weekend tradition for Columbia families. On the hunt for Halloween pumpkins? This family-owned orchard has thousands of reasonably priced options to choose from in a wide range of sizes. But pumpkins only provide the backdrop to the day's adventure. There are plenty of family-friendly outdoor activities, including hayrides, straw mazes, and hand-feeding the goats, donkeys, and rabbits. The kids will fall in love with at least one farm resident and probably beg to take it home! Bring a camera and take advantage of the artfully arranged pumpkin and gourd backdrops or the sunflower field for great family photos. Enjoy a crisp fall afternoon at Peach Tree Farms—and get a jump on your pumpkin pie.

24863 Hwy. 98, Boonville, MO, (660) 882-8009
thepeachtreefarm.com

TIP
More of a peach cobbler fan? From June through September, Peach Tree Farms sells 25 varieties of peaches at local farmers markets and from their Boonville orchard. They don't come any fresher or tastier!

FACE YOUR FEARS
AT FEARFEST

If you're looking for a little Halloween fright, FearFest can't be beat. A favorite among the teen and young-adult crowds, FearFest has sent chills down local spines for almost 20 years. The site houses four different haunted attractions: Hawthorne State Asylum, The Mortuary, Necropolis Haunted House, and Terror in the Woods, each with its own spooky-cool backstory. When you enter the attraction, you'll experience alternating periods of complete darkness, strobe lights, air blasts, loud noises, and a bit of graphic violence—but isn't that what you came for? Outside you'll see laser light shows, fireworks, and some head-banging music to get you fired up. Don't miss BLACKOUT weekend challenge, when staff link up the attractions, douse the lights, and test your navigation skills with just a glow stick!

6399 US Hwy. 40
necroplanet.com

SPORTS AND RECREATION

LET OUT A ROAR
AT FAUROT FIELD

If you want a taste of big-time college gridiron, take in a Mizzou football game at Faurot Field—a Columbia bucket list must! You can't beat the roar of the crowd on opening kickoff or the crunch of helmets against pads. My favorite thing? Tiger mania as fans tear down goalposts and haul them off to Harpo's after winning the SEC championship—well, a guy can dream, can't he? You won't find a better tailgating experience anywhere in the country. Mizzou tailgaters are known for their world-class chili, so bring a big appetite as you forage. Cornhole aficionado? There's a game on every corner. Many will welcome you to their tent for a beer and send you off with a brat—the pork kind, hopefully, and not their misbehaving offspring!

Faurot Field
600 E Stadium Blvd., (573) 882-6501
mutigers.com/sports/football

TIP
Tall, cold beverages and an average-size bladder? What do you do? Since most of the Mizzou buildings are locked, I recommend making a friend at the used RV lot—a.k.a Reactor Field—to avoid the port-o-potty lines!

TAKE REFUGE
AT SHELTER GARDENS

Want to shake off the day's stress? Step through the wrought iron gates of this vegetal oasis and leave your cares behind. Shelter Gardens, located on the Shelter Insurance grounds, is a five-acre botanical garden with over 300 different types of trees and shrubs and 15,000 annuals and perennials. Its sheer beauty makes it the perfect scenic backdrop for local photographers, picnicking families, or those seeking a relaxing stroll through nature. The gardens boast over a dozen features including a rose garden, a waterfall and reflecting pool packed with koi and goldfish, a sensory garden for the visually impaired, and a replica 19th-century one-room schoolhouse. On summer Sundays, grab a blanket or lawn chair and enjoy live music featuring local Columbia talent. The peace and quiet, the aromas, and tranquility make this a hidden gem in a bustling world.

1817 W Broadway, (573) 214-4595
shelterinsurance.com/aboutshelter/sheltergardens

HOOP IT UP
AT MIZZOU ARENA

ESPN.com called Mizzou Arena the country's finest on-campus basketball facility, and it's easy to see why. The 15,000+ seat venue is an amazing place to watch a game. The seating in the lower bowl is plush and comfortable, and 26 private suites for the uber rich circle the arena. Mizzou Arena is also home to the unofficial student "fan" group, the Antlers, a raucous and unpredictable crew of agitators that has been lauded by *Sports Illustrated* and *USA Today* for their intellectual taunts. The concessions are good, but pricey—but what stadium food isn't? Some Mizzou diehards will lament that the Hearnes Center, still standing beside its replacement, generated a better energy for the home team than Mizzou Arena. Besides basketball, Mizzou Arena has also hosted some of the best musical acts in the business: Elton John, the Eagles, Brad Paisley, and many others.

Mizzou Arena
1 Champions Dr., (573) 882-6501
mutigers.com/facilities/mizzou-arena/2

FUN FACTS

Place these in the major gaffes file. Mizzou Arena was dedicated in 2004 as Paige Sports Arena, but rebranded when it was found that "Paige," daughter of a major donor, had cheated her way through college. Oops! And in 2017, a former staffer smashed his car through arena gates, leaving $100,000 in damage—and a Volkswagen—on the court!

GET YOUR GOAT
AT FOUR OAKS FARM

Who doesn't love a goat, with its angelic face and adorable bleat? But how about a goat traipsing across your back while you're "downward dogging" it? Well, come to Four Oaks Farm and Goat Yoga of Missouri and find out. Goat yoga is relaxing and healthy—I "kid" you not! So, what is it about goats? They're cute and they make people smile. But they are also a form of animal therapy that reduces anxiety and lowers blood pressure. Combine that with the mindfulness of yoga and the scenic outdoors, and you've got an exercise that may be the G-O-A-T! Goat Yoga of Missouri requires a minimum of 15 people per class, so grab your friends and hoof it on down to Four Oaks Farm. They'll give you a memory you won't forget. Classes run from April until late October.

11805 E Judy School Rd., (573) 808-3310
fouroaksfarm.info

TIP

Besides Goat Yoga, Four Oaks Farm is a great place for the kids. Paid admission will provide kids time at their petting zoo, goat playground, hay pyramid, and pipe slide. In the fall, come pick pumpkins and wander through their sunflower fields.

MAKE IT A DAY
AT MIDWAY

Midway Golf & Games is the fun and games mecca in mid-Missouri. Midway underwent an extensive renovation in 2018 that transformed it into a true all-ages destination. Kids need something to do on the weekend? Let them loose on the outdoor 18-hole mini-golf, go-karts, batting cages, foot golf, archery tag, laser tag, corn maze, and free yard games like cornhole, Jenga, Bocce Ball, and more. As for mom and dad, they can enjoy the axe-throwing booth—it is mid-Missouri, after all—the driving range, and the 16-hole par-three golf course. The pro shop also offers a full range of golf clubs and equipment, clothing, custom club fitting, and even lessons. One visit to Midway and it will be your family's favorite stop.

5500 W Van Horn Tavern Rd., (573) 445-8100
midwaygolfgames.com

RIDE THE WIND
AT THE BALLOON FESTIVAL

Columbia was once a hot spot in the sport of ballooning, having hosted the Show-Me Balloon Challenge, the National Hot Air Balloon Championships, and others. These events drew thousands of visitors to the town and spawned a generation of balloon enthusiasts. Today amateur balloonists continue to take the short trip out to Ashland near Columbia Regional Airport for the annual Missouri Autumn Carnival and Balloon Festival. It's a four-day adventure that offers carnival rides, food vendors, hot air balloon rides, tethered rides for the squeamish, and the evening balloon illumination, or balloon glow. Watching these seven-story-high colorful balloons lined up in a row and lit up against the evening sky is truly an unforgettable sight. So, get out there and experience the world from a different perspective.

Cartwright Business & Technology Park
7070 Baldrige Ave., Ashland, MO
mohotair.com

TIP

If you are interested in giving this bucket list experience a go, try some of these local and highly experienced balloon-ride companies:

Balloon Stormers
603 N Henry Clay Blvd., Ashland, MO, (573) 814-4000
balloonstormers.com

Skyview Balloon Rides
2005 Hatton Ct., (573) 303-2261
skyviewballoons.com

Aerial Advantage Inc.
P.O. Box 838, (573) 449-1693
flyaerialad.com

GEAR UP
FOR ROCK BRIDGE

The 2,300-acre Rock Bridge State Park is a series of trails ranging from one half to seven miles in distance. All are hiking trails with varying degrees of difficulty, but some are also geared for mountain biking or horseback riding. Lace on those hiking boots for the different topography: forested areas, streams, rocky bluffs and drop offs, structural crossings, cave systems, and natural springs. The most impressive part of the park might be the trail leading to the Devil's Icebox, a cave network of over seven miles beneath a 63-foot-high natural rock bridge. Named for its year-round 56-degree temperature, the Icebox cave system still hasn't been completely explored. Bring waterproof boots and a flashlight to explore the 166-foot-long Connor's Cave and its underground waterfall and stream. Every trail offers a different experience, but each will leave you awestruck at the natural beauty residing within Columbia's borders.

5901 S Hwy. 163, (573) 449-7402
mostateparks.com/park/rock-bridge-memorial-state-park

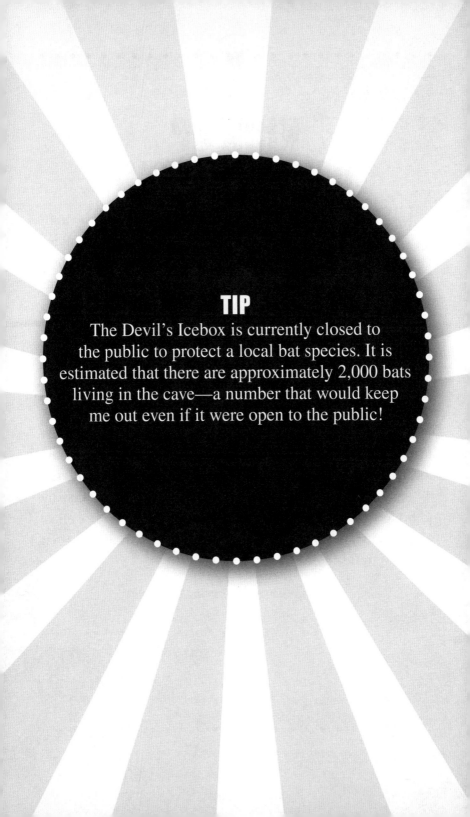

TIP

The Devil's Icebox is currently closed to the public to protect a local bat species. It is estimated that there are approximately 2,000 bats living in the cave—a number that would keep me out even if it were open to the public!

KICK UP SOME TRAIL DUST
AT KATY TRAIL STATE PARK

One of the state's greatest gifts to its residents is the Katy Trail State Park, a 240-mile rail trail from Machens, Missouri (east), to Clinton, Missouri (west). At mile marker 169 near McBaine, the 9.3-mile MKT Trail spur provides Columbia's nature and fitness enthusiasts access to the statewide trail. Running along the Missouri River's northern bank, the Katy Trail offers spectacular views of the waterway, prairie and farmland, and soaring rock faces and bluffs. Dense woodlands provide a shady leaf canopy over many trail sections, and crushed limestone makes it perfect for cyclists, joggers, hikers, and horseback riders alike. While the trail doesn't extend all the way west to Kansas City, the 47-mile Rock Island Spur gets you close. Plans are underway to bridge the final 34 miles to the City of Fountains as well as add an additional 144 miles to the Rock Island Trail east from Windsor to Beaufort.

mostateparks.com/park/katy-trail-state-park

HIKE THREE CREEKS

Located five miles south of Columbia, Three Creeks Conservation Area is a 1,500-acre nature preserve featuring unique geological formations and scenic bluffs. The area is ideal for hiking, horseback riding, and bird-watching. Make sure to hit the Turkey Creek Interpretive Trail with a one-, two-, or three-mile course, perfect for all activity levels. Wear a good pair of hiking boots for the longer loops, as you'll have to climb through rocky riverbeds and up several inclines. Don't be afraid to go off trail to examine the sinkholes, rock bluffs, and caves; it's easy to find your way back. Pick up a map in the parking lot describing the trail's checkpoints. You'll learn about plants, geological features, and even locations of land tracts given to former slaves following the Civil War.

Deer Park Rd., (573) 815-7900
mdc.mo.gov/discover-nature/places/three-creeks-conservation-area

BEAT THE HEAT
AT TWIN LAKES

Twin Lakes Recreation Area is a 73-acre mini-oasis with something for the entire family. Love to fish? Bring your poles and enjoy the stocked lake. Enjoy exercise? Stroll or jog the MKT and County House Trails. Got a mutt? Lose the leash and let them play and swim with their furry friends at the 3-acre lakeside dog park. Twin Lakes even has a separate pond and play space for smaller dogs. Hungry? Pack a lunch and enjoy the picnic tables and sheltered pavilion. Kids will love the playground, lake swimming area, and Little Mates Cove, a pirate-themed mini-water park with water cannons, slides, sprinklers, and waterfalls. Twin Lakes is a warm-weather lifesaver for families who want a break from the norm and some much-needed family time.

2500 Chapel Hill Rd., (573) 874-7460
visitcolumbiamo.com/directory/twin-lakes-recreation-area

BREAK OUT OF THE ORDINARY
AT BREAKOUT COMO

Haven't tried an escape room yet? What are you waiting for? Put your problem-solving abilities, creativity, and intelligence to the test at Breakout COMO. The rules are simple: you have 60 minutes to solve the room's mysteries to get yourself out. Breakout COMO has been around since 2016 and has gained a reputation as both challenging and entertaining. Once affiliated with top-rated Breakout KC in Kansas City, Breakout COMO is unique among the competition, with owners Jon Westhoff and Connor Hickox now designing their own breakout rooms. With five different rooms to choose from, each with a different theme and challenge level, Breakout COMO has something for everybody. Make it a date night or grab your friends for an "intelligent" night on the town!

218 N 8th St., (573) 340-5625
breakoutcomo.com

TIP

Breakout COMO only takes groups of two or more, so book a room with a few friends. Or if you're adventurous, go by yourself and get paired up with some new friends.

LET YOUR SPIRIT SOAR
AT EAGLE BLUFFS

Another of Missouri's natural wonders, Eagle Bluffs Conservation Area consists of miles of forests, glades, and wetland marshes providing year-round homes for migrating birds and wildlife. Bordering the Katy Trail State Park near McBaine, this 4,400-acre tract is the perfect spot for hiking, bird-watching, and hunting. My advice: hike the trail from the South Warren School Road parking area. You'll travel the crests of sloping, wooded hills until you reach the rocky bluff's observation deck, where an awe-inspiring visual experience awaits: magnificent views of the Missouri River, Perche Creek, the Katy Trail, and miles of fertile wetlands. Watch for bald eagles gliding on the breeze below you. From the Katy Trail at the bottom of the bluff, a short detour (keep your eye out for the sign) and a vertical hike will also lead you to this breathtaking vantage point.

Star School Rd., (573) 445-3882
mdc.mo.gov/discover-nature/places/eagle-bluffs-conservation-area

SWEAT IT OUT
AT THE ARC

The taxpayer-funded 73,000-square-foot Activities and Recreation Center (ARC) was a much needed, low-cost, community fitness facility when it opened in 2002. For 20 years, the ARC has established a welcoming environment for kids, adults, and seniors. It's like a YMCA on 'roids, with weights and cardio equipment; a youth weight training area; an elevated indoor walking/running track; a 13,000-square-foot Water Zone with a lazy river, vortex, triple loop slide, interactive water play structure, hydro-therapy pool, and three 25-meter lap lanes; group exercise classes and spinning studio; and gymnasium for volleyball, basketball, and pickleball. The ARC offers personal training and childcare, and the pool can be reserved for birthday parties. The ARC also serves its citizens as a cooling center during the humid summer months.

1701 W Ash St., (573) 874-7700
como.gov/contacts/activity-recreation-center-arc

TIP

The ARC offers very reasonable rates for youths, adults, and seniors, including day rates ranging from $3.75 to $6 and monthly passes ranging from $25 to $40. For families of up to five (two adults, three children), daily and monthly passes are $15 and $59, respectively.

KICK AXE
AT COMO AXE ATTACK

COMO Axe Attack is one of the most innovative business models and unique activities on our list. Axe throwing? Absolutely! COMO Axe has 10 throwing lanes and expert staff to help you perfect the skill of axe, knife, ninja star, and even playing card throwing! Holding an outdoor get together? COMO Axe will come to you with their mobile axe-throwing trailer. Frustrated at work? Perform your own "Axe of Rage" in their Rage Room. Take it out on computer monitors, printers, and keyboards, plates, cups, and glassware, even TVs and DVD players. Or bring your own smash-worthy items. To top it off, COMO Axe carries beverages from Logboat and Bur Oak breweries, domestic beer, wine, and mixed drinks. A great idea for parties, team building, and safe, destructive fun!

901 Safari Dr., Ste. 105, (573) 544-9130
comoaxeattack.com

JOIN THE FUN
AT SOAP BOX DERBY

In the heart of the Midwest, nothing screams "Americana" like Soap Box Derby. In this town, Mid-Missouri Soap Box Derby has been going strong for over 80 years. The rules are easy: soap box racers must have four wheels, no engines, and be gravity powered. Other than that, you're good to go. On race day, the steepest part of Broadway downtown is closed to traffic, racers are paired off and sent down a start ramp, and the race is on! Individual businesses sponsor the soap box racers, and winners are eligible to compete in the All-American Soap Box Derby in Ohio. But the Derby is about more than national attention or glory. It's a generational tradition—grandparents, parents, and kids working together and sharing time, laughter, and smiles. Maybe that's why even if you lose, it's still a win!

(573) 881-3471
midmosbd.org

CULTURE AND HISTORY

STRIKE A POSE
AT THE COLUMNS

The Columns on the Mizzou campus are one of the most popular landmarks in the state and the site of numerous university events and traditions. Standing 42 feet tall, the six Ionic limestone columns are all that remain of Academic Hall, which burned to the ground in 1892. Deemed an eyesore and safety hazard, they were on the verge of demolition until saved by a citizen protest. One-hundred-thirty years later, matriculating freshmen still pass through the columns to celebrate their entrance into university life, and graduating seniors exit through the columns to symbolize their enduring connection to the university. The Columns are the regular backdrop for graduations, weddings, photos, and selfies, while many simply choose to lounge beneath their towering splendor. Although the columns are structurally sound, renovations were conducted in 2010 and 2017 to repair hairline fractures in the base and seal cracks in the limestone.

David R. Francis Quadrangle, University of Missouri
missouri.edu/about/columns

TOUR
THE CITY'S AFRICAN AMERICAN HISTORY

The African American Heritage Trail is a two-mile loop around the city with 20 historical sites celebrating local Black leaders and institutions. Like many places, Columbia was a divided city during the era of segregation. But in a 30 square-block downtown area, a thriving community of Black-owned businesses, schools, and institutions emerged and prospered. Until 1960, that is, when a controversial urban renewal project displaced much of the community and demolished many of its homes and businesses. The Trail is a must-see educational and inspiring celebration of those who succeeded in the face of overwhelming odds. Highlights include Sharp End, the Black business and entertainment district; Cummings Academy, the first post-Civil War school for Columbia's black children; and the home of J. W. "Blind" Boone, the famed local ragtime musician and composer.

500 E Walnut St., Ste. 102, (573) 442-8303
columbiaredi.com/african-american-heritage-trail

CELEBRATE
MIZZOU HOMECOMING

Legend has it that Mizzou Homecoming is the oldest celebration of its kind in the country, dating back to 1911. But whether it was truly the first such celebration is subject to debate. Nevertheless, Mizzou's weeklong celebration each October is one of the country's largest, longest, and most entertaining homecoming events. The family-friendly festivities rev up early in the week with one of the nation's largest student-run community blood drives, student talent shows, and spirited Mizzou-themed decorations adorning downtown businesses. The party kicks into overdrive on Friday night with Spirit Rally and Greek town's legendary frat house decorations and live skits/performances. Saturday features a huge parade through downtown and morphs into a day-long tailgating party, culminating in a raucous gridiron battle under the lights. Do yourself a favor and experience this time-honored tradition.

University of Missouri
mizzou.com/s/1002/alumni/19/event.aspx?sid=
1002&gid=1001&pgid=10101

GET THE FACTS
AT THE STATE HISTORICAL SOCIETY

Opened in 2019, the Center for Missouri Studies is the headquarters of the State Historical Society of Missouri. What catches the eye first is the architecture. Missouri's winding waterways influenced the design of the signature wood staircase that greets you on the first floor, and much of the building's granite and wood was sourced from around the state. The ground floor's free gallery showcases Missouri's history through the artwork of homegrown artists like George Caleb Bingham and Thomas Hart Benton as well as over 18,000 editorial cartoons. The second-floor research center is staffed to help you navigate the over 9,000 manuscript collections, 8,000 maps, 4,800 oral history interviews, and 100,000 historical photographs, postcards, and graphics, along with the ever-expanding digital library. The Center's treasure trove of on-demand programming, workshops, lecture series, and podcasts is also accessible from your laptop.

605 Elm St., (573) 882-1187
shsmo.org

DISCOVER FRANCIS QUADRANGLE

The David R. Francis Quadrangle is a 33-acre green space in the heart of the Mizzou campus and at the epicenter of its historical roots. The Quad features the six signature limestone Columns; the domed landmark, Jessie Hall, one of a dozen other nearby buildings on the National Register of Historic Places; and Thomas Jefferson's original tombstone. But the Quad's beauty is its most enduring feature, making it a popular student lounging spot as well as the site of numerous Mizzou traditions: the Tiger Walk through the Columns to celebrate entrance into university life; Tap Day, the inclusion of select students into Mizzou's secret honorary societies; and the Francis statue "nose rub," purported to guarantee an "A" on any exam. Three nose jobs have been required to rehab the statue's worn-out proboscis, attesting to the latter tradition's popularity.

University of Missouri
410 S 6th St., (573) 882-2121
visitcolumbiamo.com/directory/francis-quadrangle

TIP

For all those green-thumbs out there, the Mizzou campus is a 735-acre botanical garden. If you stroll the Francis Quadrangle's perimeter, take a peek at the markers in front of the quad-facing buildings identifying the numerous native and non-native Missouri plants, flowers, shrubs, and trees.

DIG THE MUSEUM
OF ART & ARCHEOLOGY

Looking to get lost in history's artifacts and antiquities? You couldn't find a better place than the Museum of Art & Archeology. With a diverse collection of over 16,000 objects across 6,000 years of human history, the museum's exhibitions and programming rival the best in the Midwest. As part of Mizzou's educational mission, the museum ensures their exhibits and collections are affordable and accessible to all. The Museum also has a strong commitment to community outreach. Their "Partners in Education" program fosters lifelong art appreciation for Columbia public school students, and their "Healing Arts" program provides art therapy for adults with Alzheimer's Disease. The museum has been closed to prepare for its relocation to the main campus, but their extensive archive of online exhibitions has allowed continued access to this important historical record.

Mizzou North
115 Business Loop 70 W, (573) 882-3591
maa.missouri.edu

BEHOLD
THE BEHEMOTH BUR OAK

This massive Columbia landmark, known simply as the "big tree," is 74 feet tall with a 295-inch girth and spread of 130 feet. Not only is the McBaine Bur Oak the largest in Missouri, but it is tied for the largest such tree in the country. Recently named as a Boone County historical site, the 380-year-old oak has survived centuries of droughts, tornados, historic floods, fires, vandals, and at least six lightning strikes! Its position beside a rural road, among miles of corn fields, and 1,000 feet from the nearest tree in any direction, amplifies the oak's magnificence. The big tree has been the site of numerous weddings, funerals, and, according to local lore, several murders throughout the centuries. Sadly, the oak is in the twilight of its lifespan, so take a moment and experience this awe-inspiring sight while its majesty remains.

Bur Oak Rd.

TIP

You can get to the Bur Oak by car along Route K, about 12 miles southwest of Columbia, but there is also great access via the Katy Trail. It's about a quarter mile from the trail, making it the perfect detour for the curious.

WANDER THROUGH THE CATACOMBS
ON FIRST FRIDAYS

The North Village Arts District is a nine-square-block collection of art galleries, dance studios, music venues, coffee shops, and small businesses with a one-of-a kind energy. During the monthly First Fridays Art Walk you can witness live art demonstrations, take in live music, and peruse the amazing pottery, glass, jewelry, paintings, and wearables from the different studios and galleries that keep their doors open late. And it's all free! There are plenty of refreshments and activities for the kids, too. The fun part is wandering through the funky underground network of colorful tunnels known as "the Catacombs" that connect several of the galleries and shops. With such an eclectic mix of entertainment and local art from the area's most talented craftspeople, First Fridays Art Walk in the North Village Arts District is an unforgettable night out.

1019 E Walnut St., (573) 442-2999
northvillageartsdistrict.org/first-fridays

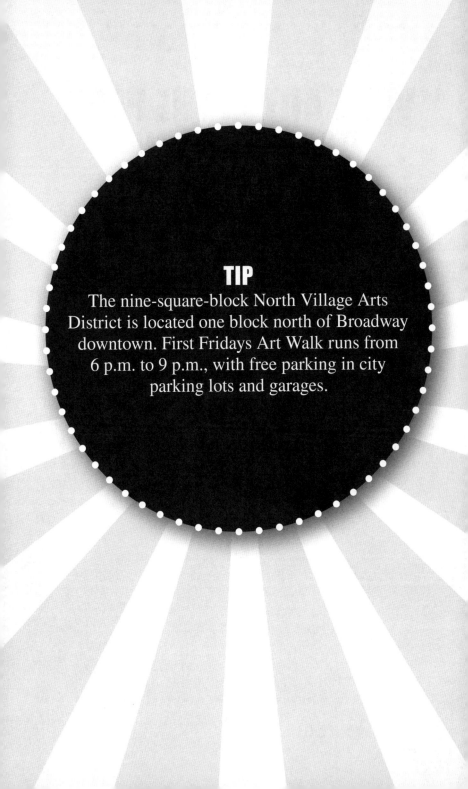

TIP

The nine-square-block North Village Arts District is located one block north of Broadway downtown. First Fridays Art Walk runs from 6 p.m. to 9 p.m., with free parking in city parking lots and garages.

VISIT ART IN THE PARK
AT STEPHENS LAKE PARK

Sponsored by the Columbia Art League, Art in the Park is a two-day, annual festival that has been supporting mid-Missouri's local artists and craftspeople since 1958. The great thing is, it's free! Held at Stephens Lake Park, the event draws over 12,000 people each year and has something for everyone. Whether you're shopping for gifts like ceramic mugs, scarves, or jewelry, or need a painting or sculpture for the home, you'll find something incredible. Visit the emerging artists' and veteran artists' tents to support mid-Missouri's up-and-coming and military talent. The kids will enjoy the caricature artists, henna tattooists, face painting, t-shirt tie-dying tent, and more. With food trucks and food tents galore, you can make a day of it. No, wait—make it a weekend and support the region's amazing artists!

Stephens Lake Park
2001 E Broadway, (573) 443-8838
columbiaartleague.org/artinthepark/home

MARVEL
AT THE MYSTERIOUS BOATHENGE

If you're ever riding your bike along the Katy Trail near mile marker 162 in Easley, keep your eyes peeled for a cryptic work of lawn art beside the "Big Muddy" near Cooper's Landing. It's a strange configuration of scuffed and dented fiberglass boats wedged vertically into the earth. Arranged to simulate Wiltshire, England's stone namesake, BoatHenge's tongue-in-cheek "shrouded in mystery" backstory is almost as entertaining as the art itself. Rumor has it, the boats either fell from the sky or sprouted from the earth after the 100-year floods of the 1990s, arranging themselves into their curious pattern. And if you believe that, I've got a half-boat to sell you . . . cheap! Make sure to stop at this quirky little novelty, a reminder that art doesn't have to take itself too seriously.

boathenge.net

ADMIRE THE HEAVENLY SPIRE
OF FIRST BAPTIST CHURCH

Although the original structure was razed and rebuilt in 1957, the First Baptist Church is notable for its massive spire aimed toward the heavens. First Baptist is not only fascinating architecturally, but also has a history as a progressive church. It was founded by William Jewell in 1823, and its members were early advocates for education and helped establish the University of Missouri, William Jewell College, and Stephens College, a private women's college. It baptized and admitted slaves as members and even "licensed" a black preacher by 1840. Long before they could vote nationally, women were involved in church committees and chaired the Board of Trustees by the turn of the 20th century. Today, the church continues its progressive mission with a woman pastor and its avid support of the LGBTQ community.

1112 E Broadway, (573) 442-1149
fbc-columbia.org

PROWL THE TIGER

Stroll through the Tiger Hotel lobby and you might think you're visiting a boutique hotel in San Francisco or Boston. The Tiger Hotel is luxurious-cool, with gold-embossed crown moldings, funky chandeliers, and original Salvador Dali art hanging in the lobby. But the Tiger provides more than just luxury accommodations. Looking for a swanky speakeasy? Head to the Vault, hidden away on the lower level. Peckish? Glenn's Café will serve you elegant Midwest fare with a twinge of Mississippi Delta along with award-winning wines. More of a craft beer, spirits, and charcuterie board fan? Belly up to the bar at Twain, their traditional taproom. You can get your fill of DJs, dancing, and live music at the Industry nightclub and satisfy your sweet tooth at their English-style candy store, May Contain Nuts. Whatever your fancy, the Tiger Hotel has it.

23 S 8th St., (573) 875-8888
thetigerhotel.com

TIP

If you're driving around Columbia searching for the Tiger Hotel, just look to the skies and follow the red "TIGER" letters perched on top of its roof. The iconic sign is something of an unofficial downtown landmark.

● ●

STROLL THE AVENUE
OF THE COLUMNS

Connecting downtown Columbia and the University of Missouri, 8th Street forms the figurative bridge between "town" and "gown." Known as the Avenue of the Columns, this historic street is flanked on the north and south ends by towering, freestanding pillars perfectly aligned with each other. To the north sit four 30-foot Doric columns preserved from a fire that gutted the Boone County Courthouse in 1909. To the south is one of the most popular landmarks in the state, the six 42-foot-tall Mizzou limestone columns, also the remnants of a building fire more than a century ago. Stroll the historic Avenue and enjoy the city's revitalization efforts: tiled stone benches, sidewalk renovations, City Hall's breathtaking steel and glass keyhole-shaped sculpture, Courthouse Plaza's relocated war memorials, and funky traffic box art featuring the work of local artists.

8th St.
visitcolumbiamo.com/directory/avenue-columns-8th-street

BRAVE
COLUMBIA'S HISTORIC BONEYARD

The Columbia Cemetery has been in use for over 200 years, expanding from its original six lots in 1821 to over 34 acres today. The cemetery reveals the town's history in each grave marker's unique epitaph and architecture. The thin, stone tablets of 18th-century grave markers with simple inscriptions and few ornamented carvings contrast with the more elaborate Victorian era's cemetery "art"—obelisks, columns, and draped urns. And the images of lambs and angels signifying a child's death, or clasped hands depicting matrimony, are both beautiful and poignant. Reflecting the practices of the times, the cemetery segregated both Jewish and African American graves. The African American Heritage Trail includes the Columbia Cemetery on its tour because at least 31 members of the US Colored Civil War Veterans are interred in this latter section. If you are searching for local history, Columbia Cemetery is a peaceful educator.

30 E Broadway, (573) 449-6320
hawthornmemorialgardens.net

FIND
THE HIDDEN JEWELL

Tucked away between a Waffle House and a housing complex sits a historic cemetery hiding in plain sight. "No one not the husband, wife or child of a descendant of George Jewell can be buried here" greets you at the Jewell Cemetery gate. The most famous of the Jewell family was William Jewell, the second mayor of Columbia, who helped establish the First Baptist Church, three colleges (including his namesake in Liberty, MO), and a city hospital. Inside the cemetery's stone boundaries, Jewell and 40 relatives are buried beneath elaborate and ornately carved headstones. Jewell family slaves are thought to be buried in two unmarked rows, only adding to the historical complexity of the Jewell legacy. Jewell Cemetery is a peaceful relic amidst the blight of suburban sprawl, and a required visit for historical enthusiasts.

S Providence Rd., (573) 449-7402
mostateparks.com/park/jewell-cemetery-state-historic-site

CHEW THE FAT
AT THE TIGER BARBER SHOP

With a swirling red, blue, and white pole spinning out front, the Tiger Barber Shop is one of a dying breed of old-school barber shops. Serving Columbia men since 1926, the shop is a welcoming space, with conversation traded between barbers and customers across all three chairs. One satisfied customer described the atmosphere as "a bunch of dudes, cutting hair and chewing the fat." But be careful: while debates about hunting and fishing are free of charge according to their menu, politics will cost you $10. Probably a good rule of thumb! True to their "Tiger" name, Mizzou sports posters and memorabilia decorate their walls—as do a few deer heads. Like other historic Columbia businesses, the shop doesn't have a website and doesn't take reservations or credit cards, so bring your local checks or cash!

118 S 9th St., (573) 449-5951

PAY HOMAGE
TO THE HALL

One of downtown Columbia's more unfortunate historical sagas involves the 106-year-old Hall Theatre. The stately venue, with its six Ionic Greek columns, has sat empty on 9th Street since losing its tenant nine years ago. Built in 1916, the 1,287-seat Hall Theatre was once a downtown hot spot, hosting stage plays, early Hollywood black-and-white silent films, and vaudeville performances. The predecessor of two other historic downtown theaters—the Missouri Theatre and the Varsity (now the Blue Note)—the Hall Theatre didn't adapt as well to changing times. By 1971, the one-film theater had become a relic, succumbing to the economics of smaller, multi-plex style movie houses. Called too expensive to renovate and too beautiful to tear down, the Hall Theatre finds itself in a strange entrepreneurial purgatory.

100 S 9th St.

BONE UP ON
BOONE COUNTY'S PAST
AT BOONE COUNTY HISTORY
AND CULTURE CENTER

The Boone County History and Culture Center recounts the region's history in the form of art gallery visuals, forgotten photographs, and bios of prominent Boone Countians. In addition, notable artifacts add to the historical context: the 18-foot "River Horse" local author William Least Heat-Moon navigated through 5,000 miles of US waterways, and the restored piano of local ragtime great, J. W. "Blind" Boone. Outside the Center, the Village at Boone Junction—four relocated Boone County homes and businesses—showcases rural life during different eras from 1818 to the 1930s. Another historic structure on-site, the sturdy, brick Maplewood House from 1877, is listed on the National Historic Register. For more "living" history, the Center hosts a Meet the Author series as well as musical concerts throughout the year.

3801 Ponderosa St., (573) 443-8936
boonehistory.org

TIP

Guided tours of the Village at Boone Junction and Maplewood House were put on hold during the COVID-19 pandemic, but the Center is hoping to resume these activities in 2022.

SHOPPING AND FASHION

DRESS UP
AT MAUDE V

Stepping into Maude Vintage Clothing and Costume is like taking a stroll through a fashion time warp. Feel nostalgic for the days of big hair and mullets? First floor. Long for the days of *Mad Men* or *Ziggy Stardust*? Second floor. Anything before that? The third-floor crow's nest. At Maude V, you can express yourself any way you want to, from zany to off-kilter to retro chic. Need a costume? Maude V can help with that, too. After 21 years in business, owner Sabrina Garcia-Rubio's passion for sustainability, recycling, and repurposing remains the foundation of her enterprise and mirrors Columbia's defining spirit. You can even join her for yoga before or after store hours. Just go in—I dare you not to come out with something fun!

9 N 10th St., (573) 449-3320
maudevintage.com

TIP
You can also find Maude V's threads at their costume booth at the Midway Antique Mall (#98 on the list).

TAKE A TRIP
TO AMISH COUNTRY

Take exit 22 off Highway 63 North in Clark to share the gravel roads with horse-drawn carriages from what seems a different era. Pass picturesque red barns and silos resting amidst swaying wheat fields. You've reached Clark Amish Community, a 15-square-mile area with over 50 family businesses, many advertising with hand-painted signs hanging from mailboxes or nailed to fence posts. You'll find the freshest flowers, milk, eggs, butter, produce, baked goods, and soaps, and if you're looking for garden-fresh, locally sourced, farm-to-table—pick a label— you won't find anything more authentic! Make sure to catch their craft auction each fall for hand-built, craftsman-quality furniture, tables, games, quilts, and rugs. If you're searching for a simpler life, at least for a day, visit Clark Amish Community.

Hwy. Y, Clark, MO
facebook.com/amishcommunityinclarkmissouri

TIP

Clark is 20 miles north of Columbia. All businesses are closed on Sundays and Christian holidays—and they are cash only! The Amish do not observe Daylight Savings Time, so do the math before you hit the road.

GIVE PEACE (NOOK)
A CHANCE

Want to shop for books, clothing, and jewelry while supporting peace, social justice, and sustainability? Then shop Peace Nook. Located below street level downtown, Peace Nook isn't just a cool store; it serves as the community resource center and social activism hub of its operator, Mid-Missouri Peaceworks. Long before it was trendy, Peace Nook sourced fair-trade products. Yeah, the place is a little cluttered and tight, but they have over 5,000 book titles, clothing, natural foods, and a variety of trinkets, jewelry, essential oils, and eco-friendly products. If you can think of it, Peace Nook probably has it. Plus, as an educational nonprofit, the store charges no taxes. So, save some money for the family while you do some good for the community!

804-C E Broadway, (573) 875-0539
blog.midmopeaceworks.org/p/peace-nook.html

BROWSE THE AISLES
AT YELLOW DOG

If you're looking for a pristine, big-box bookstore, keep walking. Yellow Dog Bookshop has all the charm (and clutter) of a New York City bookshop, with overstuffed shelves and books occasionally stacked on the floor. Owners Joe Chevalier and Kelsey Hammond's passion for the written word is evidenced by the Dog's diverse and plentiful inventory. Their holdings range from literary fiction to history to religion, and they always provide great recommendations for a wide variety of authors and genres. Try their subscription book box, where each month you'll receive a book (and gift), personally curated to your literary taste. Yellow Dog hosts author events, children's story time, and poetry nights, and anyone can drop off a box of used books for repurposing (and trade in).

8 S 9th St., (573) 442-3330
yellowdogbookshop.com

TIP

Strange but true: Yellow Dog is the second 9th Street business on our list named after a beloved canine, and almost directly across the street from the other, Sparky's Ice Cream (#9 on the list).

FIND THE HITS
AT HITT RECORDS

Nostalgic for the warmth and comfort of vinyl, cassettes, 8-track tapes, and CDs? Hitt Street's Hitt Records will take you on a magic carpet ride back to a time when a long-haired kid in a concert t-shirt stared back at you from the mirror. Their catalogue ranges from the classics to today's music, including fringe and underground genres, small labels, and independent artists that you can buy, sell, or trade. And if you miss the classic Hi-Fi equipment in your old wood-paneled basement—you remember, turntables, tape decks, shag carpets, and speakers that took up half the room—you can find gently used equipment for sale or even trade in your old stuff. It's the coolest place in Columbia to get lost for an afternoon, so don't miss Hitt Records.

10 Hitt St., (573) 777-9299
hittrecords.com

SWOOP DOWN
TO SKYLARK

This local Indie was a welcome breath of fresh air downtown when it opened its doors in 2018. Run by local novelist Alex George and business partner, Carrie Koepke, Skylark Bookshop does a lot more than sell books. They host literature and poetry readings, hold book signings with Pulitzer-prize-winning journalists and best-selling authors, and even support local writers by shelving their books. The shop is warm and inviting, the staff are knowledgeable and enthusiastic, and they can always help you find that forgotten book title by that British author . . . what's her name? Try the Skylark Reading Spa to get one-on-one literary pampering and $100 to spend on their book suggestions! *USA Today* named Skylark Bookshop one of the 30 "cool Indie bookstores" in the country . . .but we knew that already!

22 S 9th St., (573) 777-6990
skylarkbookshop.com

TIP

Owner Alex George is founder and executive director of the annual Unbound Book Festival in Columbia. His connection with award-winning authors from around the world adds to the great diversity of authors (and genres) slated for store events.

GET CRAFTY
AT BLUESTEM

When you're ready to add some hand-crafted "Wow" to your home, walls, or wardrobe, Bluestem Missouri Crafts is your one-stop shop. Since 1983, this elegant downtown gallery has carried the clay, glass, wood, metal, or fiber work of Midwest artists from the eight surrounding states, all at a price that won't break the bank. Bluestem focuses on unique works and craftsmanship, from not only nationally recognized artists, but emerging local artisans, students, and apprentices as well. Bluestem's strengths are their 38 years of experience and an uncanny ability to source the most awe-inspiring creations. The staff's knowledge and skills are evident in how they always seem to help identify the perfect item or gift for any occasion. From kitchenware to picture frames, jewelry and wearables to lighting, children's toys to holiday ornaments, Bluestem is uniquely Columbia.

13 S 9th St., (573) 442-0211
bluestemcrafts.com

TRUCK ON OVER
TO MIDWAY

If you're a fan of reality TV, Midway Truck Stop and Travel Center has a place on your Columbia bucket list. The site of Travel Channel's *Truck Stop USA* from 2011 to 2013, Midway is located "midway" between St. Louis and Kansas City at the intersection of I-70 and Highway 40. You'll find all the requisite amenities for truckers and travelers: gas, showers, and a convenience store. But the 200-acre lot also has stores selling furniture, fireworks, boots, and western wear. Throw in a diner, lounge, motel, antique mall, and daycare and you've got a glimpse of Midway's eclectic flavor. On top of that, they've hosted live music shows, lawnmower races, horse and auto shows, cow patty bingo, mud runs, and the Big 70 Challenge, a popular competitive eating contest. Midway is more than just a gas 'n go stop—it's a destination.

6401 US Hwy. 40, (573) 445-9466
facebook.com/midwayts

TIP

Think you're a competitive eater? Try the Big 70 Challenge: seven buttery biscuits, 70 ounces of sausage gravy, a side of hash browns and bacon, and 60 minutes to complete. Check out one of the only competitors to successfully complete the challenge. youtube.com/watch?v=w66tiuWZjFE&t=218s

---

SNEAK A PEEK
AT THE ANTIQUES
AT MIDWAY ANTIQUE MALL

Okay, so I already mentioned that Midway Truck Stop and Travel Center had an antique mall (#97). But with over 73,000 square feet of floor space hosting over 500 vendors, Midway Antique Mall is one of the largest in mid-Missouri and has earned its own spot on the list. For all you memorabilia junkies, Midway is the Everest of antique malls and flea markets, with aisles of comic books, records, radios, coins and collectibles, artwork, trinkets, and jewelry. Pay homage to the past while you find great deals on so many things you will never need! The staff are knowledgeable and greet you with homey Midwest charm. If you're looking for a little piece of Americana just off I-70, hop into the Midway time machine and treat yourself to something unexpected . . . and completely unnecessary!

6401 US Hwy. 40, (573) 445-0042
midwayam.com

OTHER ANTIQUE MALLS AND FLEA MARKETS

Artichoke Annie's Antique Mall
1781 Lindbergh Dr., (573) 474-2056
artichokeanniesantiquemall.wordpress.com/artichoke

Itchy's Flea Market
1907 Providence Rd., (573) 443-8275
sites.google.com/a/hauptmanns.com/itchys

Veranda Antique Mall
8650 I-70 Dr. SE, (573) 814-3600
verandaantiquemall.net

McAdams Ltd.
1501 Old Hwy. 63 S, (573) 442-3151
mcadamsltd.com

STEP UP YOUR GAME
AT BINGHAMS

For guys who are ready to step up their fashion game, Binghams is your destination clothing store. This independent, privately owned clothier has been around for 40 years and provides personal attention that you won't get in a mall or big-box store. They offer appointments, wardrobe consultation, and expert tailoring in a no-pressure environment. Binghams is about looking good, and they carry over 60 of the leading brands of clothing, shoes, and accoutrements for all occasions. Binghams is unique in that they have numerous events at the store, including regular trunk shows with different designers, bourbon and beer tasting from local craft breweries, and even book signings with local authors. Don't miss their website blog. It's wardrobe 101 for guys—and we need all the help we can get!

827 E Broadway, (573) 442-6397
binghamsclothing.com

FIND YOUR WAY
TO ALLEY A

Alley A has grown into a hot spot off the beaten path for Columbians in the know. This not-so hidden gem between Broadway and Cherry Street is the result of a 2007 revitalization effort to foster an alternative downtown business, shopping, and housing experience. Even though they are a little hard to find, the current businesses are thriving: Günter Hans's European-style pub and restaurant, featuring some of the best homemade pretzels around; Shortwave Coffee's much-sought-after small-batch roast; and Kampai, one of the hottest sushi places in town. With lots of patio seating and no cars, Alley A's secluded vibe is unmatched downtown. The butterfly mural with the words "kindness changes everything" only adds to the charm. Alley A is a harbinger of things to come downtown, and the perfect blueprint to follow.

Alley A

ACTIVITIES
BY SEASON

Each turn of the calendar brings new adventures in Columbia. Here are some ideas to consider for your seasonal to-do list.

SPRING

Catch a Flick at True/False, 48

Crack the Binding at Unbound, 56

Roll On Down to Pedaler's Jamboree, 54

Take Refuge at Shelter Gardens, 73

Get Your Goat at Four Oaks Farm, 76

Mosey On Down to the MOSY, 60

SUMMER

Watch a Flick in the Park at Cosmo Park, 58

Embrace the Barnies at Maplewood Barn Theater, 63

Rock the House at the Blue Note, 61

Gather Beside the Big Muddy, 47

Beat the Heat at Twin Lakes, 84

Join the Fun at Soap Box Derby, 89

Visit Art in the Park at Stephens Lake Park, 102

Mosey On Down to the MOSY, 60

• •

FALL

WINTER

• •

SUGGESTED
ITINERARIES

HISTORY LOVERS

FAMILY FUN

● ●

DATE NIGHT (OR DAY)

ART LOVERS

Mosey On Down to the MOSY, 60

Experience the Missouri Contemporary Ballet, 59

Visit Art in the Park at Stephens Lake Park, 102

Wander through the Catacombs on First Fridays, 100

Dig the Museum of Art & Archeology, 98

Snap to the Jazz at Murry's, 8

Catch an Indie at Ragtag, 57

Get Crafty at Bluestem, 120

Dab a Brush, Drink a Blush at The Canvas on Broadway, 50

Prowl the Tiger, 105

MUSIC LOVERS

Dig the Riffs at Roots 'N Blues, 46

Rock the House at the Blue Note, 61

Snap to the Jazz at Murry's, 8

Find the Hits at Hitt Records, 118

Mosey On Down to the MOSY, 60

Gas Up and Guzzle at Pierpont General Store, 21

Gather Beside the Big Muddy, 47

Roll On Down to Pedaler's Jamboree, 54

Get Eclectic at Fretboard, 19

Wander through the Catacombs on First Fridays, 100

• •

OUTDOOR LIFE

BANG FOR YOUR BUCK

PARTY TIME

Get Up on the Roof, 33

Guzzle Some Suds at Harpo's, 11

Roll On Down to Pedaler's Jamboree, 54

Gather Beside the Big Muddy, 47

Gas Up and Guzzle at Pierpont General Store, 21

Prowl the Tiger, 105

Toss 'Em Back at "the Berg," 4

Fill Your Growler at Flat Branch, 14

Get Your Wine On with a View at Les Bourgeois, 28

Go Underground at Broadway Brewery, 16

Paddle Over to Logboat, 13

Dig the Riffs at Roots 'N Blues, 46

Catch a Flick at True/False, 48

Let Out a Roar at Faurot Field, 72

INDEX

• •

• •